D1715985

PUBLIC SPEAKING

The Path to Success

Steven D. Cohen

cognella™
San Diego, CA

Copyright © 2011 University Readers, Inc. All rights reserved. No part of this publication may be reprinted, reproduced, transmitted, or utilized in any form or by any electronic, mechanical, or other means, now known or hereafter invented, including photocopying, microfilming, and recording, or in any information retrieval system without the written permission of University Readers, Inc.

First published in the United States of America in 2011 by Cognella, a division of University Readers, Inc.

Trademark Notice: Product or corporate names may be trademarks or registered trademarks, and are used only for identification and explanation without intent to infringe.

Author photo: Jeffry Pike copyright © President and Fellows of Harvard College

14 13 12 11 10   1 2 3 4 5

Printed in the United States of America

ISBN: 978-1-60927-806-9

www.cognella.com 800.200.3908

To my mother—
for giving me the strength
to stand on the podium in the first place

CONTENTS

Acknowledgments

I want to acknowledge my student assistants, Daniel DeFraia and Christopher Drury, for making helpful suggestions throughout the writing process. I also want to thank my friend, Thomas Wei, for partnering with me to explore the relationship between music and speech. Finally, I want to express gratitude to my talented students for inspiring me to write this book.

Preface

P ublic speaking is not really about speaking in public. Although public speaking involves sharing ideas with a group of people, it is mainly a mechanism for exercising leadership.

Public Speaking: The Path to Success introduces a unique set of powerful public speaking techniques that you can use to champion a cause that matters to you. It is organized as an action-oriented guide that you can begin using right away to become a more effective public speaker. While this book won't make you a professional public speaker overnight, it will give you the tools—and hopefully the confidence—to stand up in front of a crowd and speak powerfully.

In the pages that follow, you will learn how to:

Lead from the Podium

Your primary goal as a speaker is to lead your audience members toward a particular objective. But before you can lead, you must think like a leader, and above all, know where you want to go. The first part of this book will help you develop a leadership mindset, examine your default public speaking settings, champion your cause, and embrace the art of practice. After understanding these concepts, you will be able to exercise leadership in new and exciting ways.

Connect with Your Audience

The key to connecting with your audience members is to imagine that you are going on a first date with them. If you want them to listen to what you are saying, you must first show them that you are worth listening to. The second part of this book will help you conduct an audience analysis, manage first impressions, create a strong bond, and own the room. If you employ these ideas effectively, you will be able to impress your audience members and easily land a second date.

Use Your Voice

Like a guitar or trumpet, your voice is an instrument. You can use the musical properties of your voice to "coat" your words with emotion and take your audience members on a musical journey. The third part of this book will help you tune your voice, layer the five key musical elements, and elicit specific emotional responses from your audience. Once you master these concepts, you will be able to use your voice to produce a powerful symphony of words.

Construct Memorable Messages

If you want to construct memorable messages, you can't just write down a bunch of words and read them to your audience. You must think about where you want to take your audience members, and use words that will help you take them there. The fourth part of this book will help you use powerful language, tell moving anecdotes, and leverage repetition. After digesting these ideas, you will be able to construct messages that leave a lasting impact on your audience members.

Deliver Specialized Speeches

You can stand out from the crowd by delivering powerful impromptu speeches, persuasive speeches, and inspirational speeches. Although these types of speeches may appear challenging, you can impress your audience members by structuring your ideas in specific ways.

The fifth part of this book will introduce specific techniques to help you deliver dynamic speeches. By using these techniques, you will be able to motivate your audience members to trust you, follow you, and believe in you.

These five parts are full of practical techniques that you can use to design and deliver powerful speeches. Even if you apply just a few of these techniques to your next speech, you will dramatically improve your ability to speak powerfully from the podium and captivate your audience members.

I hope that you will use the techniques in this book to pursue your passion and support a cause that really matters. Now is the time to use your voice to change minds and change hearts. Now is the time to *lead*.

Part 1

Leading from the Podium

The Leadership Mindset

E very time you deliver a speech, you are, in fact, leading. Whether you are a student, an executive, a politician, or a professor, you must lead your audience toward a particular objective. Your job isn't simply to communicate ideas to your audience members. Your job is to show them that you are a *leader*.

Your audience members won't remember everything that you say, but they will remember what they thought of you. This is why it is important that you develop the mindset of a leader. With the proper mindset, you will be able to convince your audience members that you care about them and that you want to help them achieve their goals.

To get your audience members on your side, it is essential that they trust you—trust that you believe in your message and trust that you will do what you say you will do. You can't expect your audience members to give you the benefit of the doubt. You must earn their trust by conveying the appropriate character or *ethos*.

In *The Essential Guide to Rhetoric*, William Keith and Christian Lundberg emphasize the importance of establishing credibility:

> Ethos is not automatic. Think about cases where you weren't persuaded by a speaker; if you felt the speaker wasn't honest or didn't have your best interests in mind, you might have decided not to listen to all the (potentially good) arguments presented to you.[1]

According to Keith and Lundberg, speakers can create a positive ethos by highlighting "the history of their actions, as politicians often do when invoking their voting records," referring to "deeds that exemplify their character ... [such as] a war record or participation in a social movement," and citing "their education or the research they have done with experts."[2] Ultimately, they must provide compelling reasons that their audience should believe what they are saying and consider their point of view.

Your audience members won't trust you just because you rattle off a list of impressive facts or accomplishments. They will only trust you if you think and act like a leader. By developing a leadership mindset, you will be able to create a powerful ethos that makes your audience members want to listen to you. Once you have their attention, you will be able to take them on an experiential journey—a journey that excites their minds and teaches them something about the world or about themselves.

Stepping Back

We already have established that your primary goal as a speaker is to show your audience members that you are a leader. As part of this process, you must think about how your audience members perceive you when you are standing in front of the room. You can achieve this perspective by stepping back and getting on the balcony.

Ronald Heifetz and Martin Linsky talk about the importance of "getting off the dance floor and going to the balcony" to emphasize the need for leaders to step back in the middle of a situation and ask themselves, "What's really going on here?":[3]

> Let's say you are dancing in a big ballroom with a balcony up above. A band plays and people swirl all around you to the music, filling up your view. Most of your attention focuses on your dance partner, and you reserve whatever is left to make sure that you don't collide with dancers close by. You let yourself get carried away by the music, your partner, and the moment. When someone later asks you about the dance, you exclaim, "The band played great, and the place surged with dancers."
>
> But if you had gone up to the balcony and looked down on the dance floor, you might have seen a very different picture. You would have noticed all sorts of patterns. For example, you might have observed that when slow music played, only

some people danced; when the tempo increased, others stepped onto the floor; and some people never seemed to dance at all. Indeed, the dancers all clustered at one end of the floor, as far away from the band as possible. On returning home, you might have reported that participation was sporadic, the band played too loud, and you only danced to fast music.

Achieving a balcony perspective means taking yourself out of the dance, in your mind, even if only for a moment. The only way you can gain both a clearer view of reality and some perspective on the bigger picture is by distancing yourself from the fray. Otherwise, you are likely to misperceive the situation and make the wrong diagnosis, leading you to misguided decisions about whether and how to intervene.[4]

Once you are on the balcony, you will be able to see yourself clearly. As Heifetz and Linsky explain, the "balcony" is not just a place where you can observe others; it is, perhaps more importantly, a place where you can observe yourself.[5] Getting on the balcony will help you analyze your own actions and observe how your audience members respond to you.

One of the most important ways to become a powerful public speaker is to evaluate your performance objectively. You will be able to achieve this objectivity from the balcony by noticing "that part of yourself that others would see if *they* were looking down from the balcony."[6] In fact, you will be able to understand, perhaps for the first time in your life, *how* you can improve.

There are many different ways to get on the balcony. You can pause for a moment during your speech and mentally note how your audience members are reacting to what you are saying. You also can ask a few people for feedback after your speech or videotape and review a particular speech on your own. But thinking and analyzing are the easy parts. The hard part is changing your behavior the next time you speak. Heifetz and Linsky emphasize that "staying on the balcony in a safe observer role is as much a prescription for ineffectuality as never achieving that perspective in the first place."[7]

Indeed, powerful public speaking, much like leadership, is an "improvisational art" because it requires speakers to constantly assess and improve their performance.[8] Heifetz and Linsky describe this process:

> Going back to our metaphor, you have to move back and forth from the balcony to the dance floor, over and over again … You take action, step back and assess the results of the action, reassess the plan, then go to the dance floor and make the next move. You have to maintain a diagnostic mindset on a changing reality.[9]

Stepping onto the balcony allows you to feel the emotion and capture the energy in the room. From the balcony, you can focus on what is actually happening rather than on what you are saying. Once you more firmly understand what your audience sees, you can take action steps to improve your performance.

In order to use the balcony technique to your advantage, you must know what behaviors to look for. I call these behaviors default public speaking settings.

Default Public Speaking Settings

E ach of us has default settings—automatic, pre-programmed behaviors that are comfortable and familiar. For example, when someone sneezes, our typical response is "Bless you." We don't often stop to think about why we say "Bless you." We just say it. After all, saying "Bless you" feels "right." When it comes to public speaking, however, some of our default settings may actually be impeding our ability to make a powerful impact on our listeners.

Let's try an experiment. Put down this book for a moment and clasp your hands together by interlocking your fingers as if you are praying. How does your grip feel? Comfortable, right? Normal, hopefully. Now, unclasp your hands, and clasp your hands together the *other* way, so that the opposite thumb is now on top. How does your grip feel now? A little awkward?

We each have a default way of clasping our hands—a pre-programmed grip that feels "right"—just like we each have default ways of getting dressed in the morning, preparing certain meals, and walking from one place to another. Similarly, we each have default public speaking settings—ingrained ways of communicating and interacting with our audience members.

To become a powerful public speaker, you must identify your default public speaking settings and determine the impact that they are having on your capacity to lead. By getting on the balcony, you will be able to see "your own default [ways] of interpreting and responding to events around you … and gain greater latitude and freedom to respond in new and useful ways."[10]

As you observe yourself from the balcony, make a list of the default public speaking settings that are hindering your ability to speak powerfully. Do you nervously adjust your glasses or run your hands through your hair? Do you say "um" or "uh" every few words? Do you clasp your hands in front of your body or behind your back? Once you identify these default settings, you can begin challenging yourself to adjust them.

It is worth noting that adjusting default public speaking settings isn't an easy process; it's a lot like undergoing an orthodontic procedure to eliminate a gap, straighten crooked teeth, or correct an overbite. The process may take time and the changes may feel uncomfortable for awhile, but most people would agree that the result is well worth the effort.

Although you may have many problematic default public speaking settings, you don't have to adjust them all at once. You can make significant progress by pushing yourself to overcome nervousness, eliminate filler words, and use natural gestures.

Overcoming Nervousness

Most speakers are not naturally at ease in front of an audience. In fact, many people are downright afraid of speaking in public. But when you ask these people why they feel nervous, you quickly learn that they are afraid of what *might* happen. The truth is, most of the preconceived notions that people have about public speaking stem from uncertainty about what their colleagues or friends may think of them after they finish speaking.

The only way to deal with this uncertainty is to step up. You must face any fear that you have, even the fear of being in the spotlight, because public speaking is not really about being in the spotlight. On the contrary, it is about self-sacrifice. It is about using your voice to say something that really matters.

The next time you start to feel nervous, try using a technique called the "T Repeater." Take a deep breath in and then exhale short "T" sounds very slowly until you are out of air. Go ahead. Try it. Breathe in and exhale, "Tuh-Tuh-Tuh-Tuh-Tuh-Tuh-Tuh-Tuh." Focus on relaxing your mind and your shoulders as you are exhaling. Try to make sure that your short "T" sounds are evenly spaced. Feel yourself releasing your nervousness as you let out one short "T" sound after another.

Another technique that you may want to consider is turning your palms up. You tend to be more nervous when your palms are face down next to the sides of your body. If you turn your palms up, you are less likely to have sweaty palms. So before you speak, turn your palms up, breathe in slowly, and then breathe out slowly. Repeat this exercise a few times. Then walk to the front of the room and dazzle your audience.

If you are especially nervous about speaking in front of an audience, you may want to try easing into eye contact. Many speakers believe that they have to look at their audience members right away. In reality, speakers need only create the *impression* that they are looking at their audience members. To create this effect, look at the space between an audience member's eyes or the lower part of her forehead. If there is some space between you and your audience, you also can look at the top of an audience member's head or the rims of his glasses. Shift your eye contact every few seconds just as you would if you were looking directly at individual audience members. You can use this technique until you are comfortable enough to make genuine eye contact with your audience.

Of course, these exercises will only help you overcome your last-minute jitters if you are prepared. Some speakers are nervous when they are getting ready to speak because they are not sure what they are going to say or how their speech is going to turn out. This is why it is so important that you know your material and know it well.

Eliminating Filler Words

Once you overcome your nervousness, you will be able to focus on one of the most common default public speaking settings—the use of filler words.

Why do we use filler words? The simplest answer is that we have been conditioned to answer questions immediately from an early age. When our mother or father asked a question, we were sure to answer right away—either because we wanted to show respect or because we were afraid of getting in trouble. Consequently, we feel the urge to speak when spoken to.

Some people argue that filler words are so common in everyday speech that they are generally accepted. But just because filler words may seem "natural" does not mean that they belong in formal speeches. After all, many people find filler words extremely distracting and equate the use of filler words with a lack of preparation or capability. Powerful public speakers work hard to eliminate words such as "um," "uh," "well," "so," "you know," "er," and "like" from their vocabulary so that their listeners are able to focus solely on their message.

There are two places where filler words commonly appear: at the beginning of a statement and in between ideas. See what happens the next time you are asked a question. You probably will say "um" or "uh" right away without even thinking. Then when you are finished discussing your first idea, you are likely to fill the silence with another filler word before transitioning to your next idea. You can think of these two "filler word hot spots" in the context of a two-paragraph essay. The first hot spot would be the tab before the first paragraph and the second hot spot would be the white space between the first and second paragraphs.

When you use a filler word such as "um," you are thinking verbally. In other words, you are verbalizing your thought process. Armed with this information, it is easy to realize that the best way to avoid using filler words is to *pause*. If you're not speaking, you can't say "um"! Instead of speaking right away, take a couple seconds to think about what you want to say. Then begin speaking. Pause, think, answer.

The same technique applies when you're transitioning from one idea to another. While you may be tempted to fill the silence between ideas with a filler word, remember to pause and give yourself a moment to think about what you want to say next. Don't begin speaking until you are ready. Remember: Pause, think, answer.

It may feel unnatural to pause, especially because you've been thinking aloud for your entire life. I assure you, however, that you will deliver more powerful speeches and reduce your chance of using filler words if you give yourself time to think.

If you need help overcoming a filler word problem, ask a family member, friend, or colleague to point out when you say "um" or "uh." You also may want to wear a rubber band so that you can snap yourself every time you use a filler word. I don't want you to hurt yourself; I want you to stop using filler words!

Although we live in a fast-paced society that seemingly demands instant answers, we must use the pause to our advantage. We may feel pressure to answer right away, but ultimately, we should only speak when we are ready.

Using Natural Gestures

Now that we have discussed a verbal default public speaking setting, let's turn our attention to a common nonverbal setting—the use of distracting hand gestures.

Many speakers default to crossing their arms, playing with their wedding ring, or putting their hands behind their back because they are unsure how to use their hands to their advantage. Although these behaviors may seem harmless, they can dramatically change the way that your audience members interpret your message. If you don't know what to do with your hands, leave them by your sides. But if you want to use your hands to enhance your speech, then you must learn how to gesture naturally.

Gestures are nonverbal extensions of your speech that emphasize the particular ideas that you are sharing verbally. They are important nonverbal tools that narrow the distance between you and your audience. When you reach out toward your audience members, you are physically getting closer to them. You also are conveying your emotions in a more direct and personal way.

Given the importance of gestures, you may feel tempted to insert them at particular points in your speech. However, you shouldn't try to time your gestures. Instead, you must give yourself permission to gesture naturally and purposefully.

In *There's No Such Thing as Public Speaking*, Jeanette and Roy Henderson explain that the best gestures aren't planned:

> When the image is strong enough and the point important enough, your gesture center will automatically provide the uncontrollable urge to gesture, as well as the appropriate gesture to express that image. The best rule of thumb for gestures is simply to just *wait for it*, then when you feel it, *go for it*! Eventually, with experience, you will never need to consciously think about your gestures again.[11]

It is important to feel rather than plan your gestures so that they naturally align with your words. Planned gestures look canned and insincere and often distract your audience members from what you are saying. Give yourself permission to gesture, and you will produce powerful, purposeful gestures every time.

Championing Your Cause

In order to mobilize your audience members to support a particular cause, you cannot simply speak about it; you must champion it. You may want to convince your employees to use public transportation, encourage your peers to vote in an upcoming election, or motivate your colleagues to support a nonprofit organization. Whatever your cause, you must stand up and fight for it.

At the 2008 Theodore H. White Lecture on Press and Politics at Harvard Kennedy School, Congressman John Lewis spoke passionately about the African American struggle for equality and the importance of fighting for change:

> As a nation and as a people we have come a distance, and I must tell you that I'm so deeply touched to be invited to be here ...
>
> For hundreds of years there has been a people struggling and believing, pressing and praying, sacrificing and dying in the hopes that they could bring this nation to this moment and beyond ...
>
> And people only believe, you have to have hope, you have to have faith that nothing else will do, you have to believe that it can be done. People told us that we wouldn't make it from Selma to Montgomery, that we wouldn't get our Voting Rights Act passed, that we wouldn't get a Civil Rights Act,

but we didn't give up, and we must never, ever give up. There may be some disappointments, some interruptions, some setbacks, but you keep pushing, you keep moving, and that's what people must do, and not just for ourselves.[12]

As Congressman Lewis explains, you must champion your cause no matter how difficult the journey ahead may appear. You must "keep pushing" and "keep moving" forward until you achieve something that really matters.

Addressing Three Key Questions

After identifying a cause that matters to you, you must think about the answers to three key questions to help your audience members understand how and why they should support it:

- Why is the cause important?
- What can others do to help?
- Why is it essential to act right now?

When Senator Hillary Clinton decided to suspend her presidential campaign, she had to convince millions of followers to support Senator Barack Obama—a man who was her chief Democratic rival in the 2008 U.S. presidential campaign. She was able to champion the importance of electing Senator Obama as the 44th president of the United States by addressing the three key questions in her concession speech:

> I entered this race because I have an old-fashioned conviction that public service is about helping people solve their problems and live their dreams. I've had every opportunity and blessing in my own life, and I want the same for all Americans. And until that day comes, you'll always find me on the front lines of democracy, fighting for the future.

The way to continue our fight now, to accomplish the goals for which we stand is to take our energy, our passion, our strength, and do all we can to help elect Barack Obama, the next President of the United States. Today, as I suspend my campaign, I congratulate him on the victory he has won and the extraordinary race he has run. I endorse him and throw my full support behind him. And I ask all of you to join me in working as hard for Barack Obama as you have for me ...

We may have started on separate journeys, but today our paths have merged. And we're all heading toward the same destination, united and more ready than ever to win in November and to turn our country around, because so much is at stake. We all want an economy that sustains the American dream, the opportunity to work hard and have that work rewarded, to save for college, a home and retirement, to afford that gas and those groceries, and still have a little left over at the end of the month, an economy that lifts all of our people and ensures that our prosperity is broadly distributed and shared.

We all want a health care system that is universal, high-quality and affordable so that parents don't have to choose between care for themselves or their children or be stuck in dead-end jobs simply to keep their insurance ... We cannot let this moment slip away. We have come too far and accomplished too much.[13]

Senator Clinton effectively addresses each of the three key questions. She explains why the cause is important: "We all want an economy that sustains the American dream, the opportunity to work hard and have that work rewarded ... We all want a health care system that is universal, high-quality and affordable so that parents don't have to choose between care for themselves or their children ..." She articulates what others can do to help: "The way to continue our fight now, to accomplish the goals for which we stand is to take our energy, our passion, our strength, and do all we can to help elect Barack Obama, the next President of the United States." And she emphasizes why it is essential to act right now: "We cannot let this moment slip away. We have come too far and accomplished too much."

Notice that Senator Clinton doesn't focus on herself or her own ambitions. Despite her obvious disappointment, she exudes leadership by focusing on the cause itself—the need to "turn our country around, because so much is at stake." By clearly answering each of the three key questions, Senator Clinton convinces her supporters to rally behind Senator Obama and continue to fight for change.

Finding Your Passion

If you want to be a leader, you must champion a cause that energizes you and motivates you to speak out. You can't simply tell your audience that you are passionate about a particular cause; you have to demonstrate that you are passionate about it.

But how do you know if you are passionate or driven to succeed? Randy Komisar explains this distinction in *The Monk and the Riddle*:

> Passion pulls you toward something you cannot resist. Drive pushes you toward something you feel compelled or obligated to do. If you know nothing about yourself, you can't tell the difference. Once you gain a modicum of self-knowledge, you can express your passion. But it isn't just the desire to achieve some goal or payoff, and it's not about quotas or bonuses or cashing out. It's not about jumping through someone else's hoops. That's drive.[14]

The distinction between passion and drive is very important. You are driven to get promoted. You are driven to get a project done on time. You are driven to get ahead. But you are not passionate about these objectives. Unlike drive, passion is a magnetic force that *pulls* you toward a specific goal or idea.

To discover your passion, think about what excites you the most, what makes your heart race and your mind work, what inspires you to want to change the world. You will earn your audience members' trust if you share this passion with them. If your cause has a magnetic, palpable effect on you, your audience is more likely to find the cause compelling.

At the beginning of the semester, I ask my students to stand in the center of the speaking area and introduce themselves to the class. Some students really struggle with this exercise and offer bland introductions. Here is an example:

> My name is Susan. I've been in school for a couple years now, but I'm nearing the end of the road. I come from a large family in central New York and found my way here after living in a bunch of places. So, yeah. That's about it.

It's not that students like Susan don't have anything interesting to say; they just don't know what to say. I often help these students by suggesting that they speak about something they love to do. It could be playing soccer, volunteering in the community, spending time with their kids, or traveling to foreign countries. When the students begin again, they instantly become more animated. The audience members sense this excitement and energy and become much more interested in the topic.

When you speak about something that you love, you will feel more at ease and more connected with your audience. Of course, there may be times when you have to speak about mundane topics such as tax code revisions or safety procedures. However, you will still be able to champion your cause effectively if you passionately convey why the cause is important, what others can do to help, and why it is essential to act right now.

Embracing Difficult Topics

Not every cause that you believe in will be easy to sell. At times, you may have to deliver speeches about controversial or unpopular ideas.

Picture yourself as a doctor sitting in the audience at a medical conference. You've patiently sat through four hours of presentations on everything from migraines to multiple sclerosis. Now it's finally time for your long-awaited favorite—a session on the latest advances in osteoporosis treatment.

The first of two speakers, a well-respected orthopedic surgeon, begins by giving a little bit of background on the disease itself. He then offers a wealth of information about the latest treatment options approved by the U.S. Food and Drug Administration. He presents interesting data on a variety of drugs, but he rarely offers an opinion of his own. You write down some compelling facts when he completes his presentation and then patiently await the next speaker.

The second speaker, a well-known internist, uses her PowerPoint slides mostly as background information, which allows her to speak freely. She candidly discusses the challenges of treating patients with osteoporosis and offers her perspective on allowing late-stage patients to access experimental drugs. She acknowledges that experimental drugs are unproven, but argues that patients with few alternatives should be able to access these drugs even if they may not work. Your argumentative side is piqued, and something inside you makes you want to challenge a few of her points. Nevertheless, you respect her immensely for delivering an informative, thought-provoking presentation.

Although both speakers delivered strong presentations, the second speaker exercised leadership by speaking candidly about a difficult topic. She discussed her perspective on allowing patients with late-stage osteoporosis to access experimental drugs despite the fact that not everyone would agree with her. She could have selected a "safer" topic, but instead, she spoke about a topic that she believed in, even though that it was likely to generate a little bit of controversy.

Addressing difficult topics isn't easy. In fact, it is one of the most challenging parts of public speaking. But powerful public speakers don't shy away from difficult topics; they embrace difficult topics. They continue to advocate their views firmly, but respectfully.

Dan O'Hair, Hannah Rubenstein, and Rob Stewart emphasize the importance of respecting the values of the audience when discussing a difficult topic:

> Conflicting values make it difficult to speak about certain topics without challenging cherished beliefs ... As you prepare speeches on controversial topics, anticipate that audience members will hold a range of values that will differ not only from your own, but from each other's. Demonstrate respect for your audience's values, even when you do not share them."[15]

The next time you are faced with a difficult topic, don't avoid it just because some people are unlikely to agree with you. Instead, think about how you can address the topic candidly and respectfully.

The Art of Practice

P owerful public speakers often seem magical. They have an incredible ability to impress their audience members and convey leadership ability each and every time they speak. Powerful public speakers resemble magicians because they are able to elicit specific reactions and produce surprising results.

The key to creating this magic is to treat every speech as a conversation between two people—a speaker and a listener. Jeanette and Roy Henderson explain that public speaking is not all that different from a one-on-one conversation:

> No matter how many people we are speaking to, no matter what the venue or medium, every time we speak, we should speak as though we are speaking to one person, and one person only. Once you get that into your head, the rest is so much easier.
>
> Whatever your politics, consider for a moment the speeches that were made by President Ronald Reagan. Yes, they were speeches, yet they never felt like speeches. It felt like he was in our living room having a private conversation with us. That is the goal of the perfect presentation; to realize that the number of people listening is irrelevant, you are simply having a one-on-one conversation with a lot of people at once.[16]

President Reagan was not born with the ability to make his audience members feel like he was speaking directly to them. He had a lot of time to practice—as an actor, as president of the Screen Actors Guild, as a spokesman for General Electric, as governor, and finally, as a candidate for president. President Reagan kept honing his public speaking skills until he could stand up before a large crowd and make every single person feel like he or she was the most important person in the room. President Reagan wasn't just a leader; he was a magician, a magician who earned the nickname "The Great Communicator."

If you want to become a powerful communicator, you must always imagine yourself speaking *to* someone. Don't just talk to a wall or a room full of empty seats. Practice in front of a mirror, or better yet, a family member or friend. Your goal is to make sure that your audience members *receive* your words, not just hear them.

I hope by now you have realized that people are not born with the ability to dazzle an audience. Think about an artist's ability to paint an impressive portrait. Great painters aren't born with the ability to create masterpieces. They learn about and experiment with different combinations of line, color, composition, balance, and contrast. Behind every great painting, there is a talented artist—a magician who has spent thousands of hours refining her craft.

In *Outliers*, Malcolm Gladwell discusses the "10,000-Hour Rule," a concept supporting the notion that "excellence at performing a complex task requires a critical minimum level of practice."[17] Gladwell suggests that people who have become among the best at their craft have logged about 10,000 hours of practice. He asserts that what "distinguishes one performer from another is how hard he or she works. That's it. And what's more, the people at the very top don't work just harder … than everyone else. They work much, *much* harder."[18]

Renowned neurologist Daniel Levitin supports Gladwell's assertion:

> In study after study, of composers, basketball players, fiction writers, ice skaters, concert pianists, chess players, master criminals, and what have you, this number comes up again

and again ... It seems that it takes the brain [10,000 hours] to assimilate all that it needs to know to achieve true mastery.[19]

You cannot expect to master anything—cooking, writing, chess, or mathematics—unless you do it all the time. Consequently, the only way to become a powerful public speaker is to embrace the art of practice. You must make public speaking a hobby by seeking opportunities to speak. Ask to introduce a keynote speaker. Volunteer to speak at a company function. Sign up for a role at a local Toastmasters meeting. It doesn't matter where you speak. What matters is that you keep pushing yourself to speak in public, no matter how many times you make mistakes.

It may seem nearly impossible to amass 10,000 hours of public speaking "experience" especially when you realize that you would have to make speaking your full-time job for the next five years to even reach 10,000 hours. But one important fact remains. If you commit to speaking wherever and whenever you can—at work, at school, even at home—you *will* get better.

Discussion Questions

1. Why is it important to develop a leadership mindset?
2. Why is public speaking an "improvisational art"?
3. How can you identify your default public speaking settings?
4. Why are many people afraid of speaking in public?
5. What are "filler word hot spots"?
6. What does it mean to "give yourself permission" to gesture naturally?
7. How can you champion a cause effectively?
8. What is the difference between passion and drive?
9. How should you address difficult topics?
10. How can you amass public speaking "experience"?

PART 2

CONNECTING WITH YOUR AUDIENCE

Knowing Your Audience

B efore you can lead your audience, you must *know* your audience. You must understand what your audience members care about and why they are willing to listen to you in the first place.

The best way to get to know an audience is to conduct an audience analysis. Dan O'Hair, Hannah Rubenstein, and Rob Stewart define an audience analysis as "the process of gathering and analyzing information about audience members' attributes and motivations with the *explicit aim of preparing your speech in ways that will be meaningful to them.*"[1] By maintaining an "audience-centered approach" throughout the speech preparation process, speakers will ensure that their audiences will want to listen to their speeches.[2]

You should begin the audience analysis process by thinking about whom you will be addressing. Don't spend too much time collecting demographic information (such as your audience members' gender, age, and occupation) since these characteristics are only marginally useful. Instead, gather as much information as you can about what you have in common with your audience members and what they have in common with one another. Focus on interests, goals, and passions, not demographics.

After the first two weeks of class, I challenge my students to conduct an audience analysis so that they can tailor their upcoming speeches to the people who will be listening to them. One student described his audience as follows:

The students come from all over the nation and world—Kim, an older Australian woman who speaks softly but sings high notes with ease; Gagan and Jonathan from Canada; Daniel, a tall tenor who took a bus from the Midwest; Francine, a fashion writer and graduate student from San Diego; and Isabel from Portugal. The small gathering includes young and old, female and male, undergraduates, graduate students, and even some students who are themselves professors and teaching assistants. Brazilian, Southern American, and English accents vary the timbre of class discussions. Passions vary, too. Scott loves financial markets, and Cara is passionate about the environment. A speaker's challenge, therefore, is to find what unites this motley assemblage and build on a common basis of understanding. To say we are united by public speaking is too broad; the class includes both those who fear it and those who relish it. We are united specifically by our belief that it is *important*. We know that the spoken word has power, and whether it is manifest in corporate boardrooms or pulpits, we want to use that power to improve our corners of the world.[3]

This audience analysis is effective because the student is able to connect his beliefs with his audience members' beliefs. Although the student acknowledges the tremendous diversity of the audience, he doesn't dwell on it. He quickly focuses on what unites everyone in the room—"our belief that [public speaking] is *important*." He thinks deeply about what he has in common with his audience members and what they have in common with one another: "We know that the spoken word has power, and whether it is manifest in corporate boardrooms or pulpits, we want to use that power to improve our corners of the world."

Admittedly, you may not have a full two weeks to research your audience before working on your speech. However, the importance of getting to know your audience members before speaking to them cannot be overstated. Conduct some online research to learn more about your audience members, or ask the event organizer to tell you more about their interests and concerns. Then use the information that you have gathered to think about what you have in common with your audience members and what they have in common with one another. Once you feel as though you know your audience members, you will feel prepared to meet them and make a solid first impression.

Managing First Impressions

T he most effective way to make a positive impression on your audience members is to do everything you can up front to make them like you. This idea may surprise you, given that public speaking seems to be focused on the process of designing and delivering messages. But the truth is that the more your audience members like you, the more likely they are to listen to what you have to say.

I often talk to my students about the importance of taking their audience on a first date. Of course, I don't mean that they should ask their audience members out on actual dates. I mean that they should prepare for their speech in the same way that they would prepare for a first date. In doing so, they will maximize the possibility that their audience members will like them and want to listen to them.

It is important to remember that your "first date" with your audience begins long before you utter the first word. As soon as your audience members see you, they will begin evaluating you based on how you look, what you do, and how you carry yourself. They may not have a lot of data on which to form their conclusions, but they will find it relatively easy to form an impression of you. This is why it is essential that you learn how to manage first impressions.

You may find it shocking that your audience members can develop an impression of you without knowing anything about you or what you plan to say. However, Malcolm Gladwell reminds us that thin-slicing—the inherent ability to make quick decisions based on very little information—is a natural part of our everyday decision making:

> Thin-slicing is not an exotic gift. It is a central part of what it means to be human. We thin-slice whenever we meet a new person or have to make sense of something quickly or encounter a novel situation. We thin-slice because we have to, and we come to rely on that ability because there are lots of hidden fists out there, lots of situations where careful attention to the details of a very thin slice, even for no more than a second or two, can tell us an awful lot.[4]

Think of thin-slicing as an intuitive response to any type of stimulus. For example, when you hear a new song on the radio, look at a picture on a wall, or listen to a politician on the campaign trail, you automatically have a *feeling* about what you are hearing or seeing. This initial feeling forms the basis of your opinion.

Your audience members will form an opinion of you within seconds of seeing you for the first time. While you may not be able to control their first impression, you certainly can influence it by knowing how to project authority and greet your audience.

Projecting Authority

Some authors define "public speaking" as a process featuring a speaker who delivers a message and an audience that is attentive during the delivery of the speech. This definition is problematic, however, because it implies that the audience will listen to a speaker just because he is standing in front of the room. In reality, a speaker must convince his audience members that he is worthy of their time and attention.

Remember that your audience members will begin to thin-slice you as soon as they see you. Consequently, you must project authority to show them that you are an important speaker with an important message.

One way to project authority is to select an outfit that makes you look like a leader. You want to look important without appearing inaccessible. As Jeanette and Roy Henderson explain, you can achieve this balance by selecting an outfit that is "one step above" what your audience members will be wearing:

> For example, for men, when the attire of the [audience] is jeans and a T-shirt, you should wear something like casual slacks and a collared pullover shirt. When the [audience] will be wearing casual slacks and a dress shirt, you should wear something like dress pants and a sports jacket. When the [audience] is in suit and tie, you should be in a better suit, perhaps vested and with a beautiful silk tie. For women, the strategy is the same. When your [audience] is in jeans, you should wear dress pants or a casual dress. When your [audience] is in dress pants, you should be wearing a nice suit or a more tailored dress, and so on.
>
> Always dress "one step up" and your authority will be supported by your attire. Simply stated, you want your clothes to say, "I'm just like you, I just have a little more knowledge or authority. Therefore, I've been a little more successful on this particular subject."[5]

If you're not sure what your audience members will be wearing, ask the event organizer or stop by the venue in advance to get a sense of how people dress. You want to make sure that you "fit in" with your audience members so that they will perceive you as an important, yet accessible leader.

Another way to project authority is to act like a leader as soon as you arrive at the venue. Remember that your audience members will begin evaluating your leadership ability as soon as they see you. Don't let this attention worry you. Hold your head high, smile when you first meet someone, and make direct eye contact when you are engaged in a conversation. Use every interaction as a chance to make your audience members like you before you begin speaking.

As Shel Leanne notes, speakers who exude trust and confidence make a strong first impression on others:

> People know charisma when they see it—that certain fire in the eye, passion and command … Adept leaders capitalize on that first defining moment. Through skillful use of body movement and image, they start a two-way dialogue of sorts, making excellent impressions that last. This helps establish a firm foundation for commanding authority and wielding leadership.[6]

This "two-way dialogue" is especially important when other people are speaking. Your audience members will be looking at you to see if you are paying attention to the people speaking before you. If you sense that people are looking at you, don't look back at them; instead, stay focused on the speaker. You can enhance your image by showing your audience members that you are interested in what other people are saying.

You also can enhance your image by having someone introduce you before you begin speaking. As Jeanette and Roy Henderson note, "the [audience] will see that you are important enough to *have* someone introduce you, which has a credibility factor all its own, and will respond with suitable respect for your position."[7] During the introduction, your audience members will be looking at you while the speaker is discussing your accomplishments. You can briefly make eye contact with your audience, but for the most part, you should stay focused on the person introducing you, even if you know what he is going to say. Remember: You want to show your audience members that you care about what other people are saying.

One of the major benefits of projecting authority before your speech is that you already will be in the right mindset when you walk to the center of the speaking area. You will look like a leader and feel like a leader. The next step is to demonstrate that you *are* a leader.

Greeting Your Audience

An easy, but powerful way to make a positive first impression on your audience members is to greet them before you begin speaking. If you greet your audience members properly, you will make them feel welcome and important.[8]

The first step is to approach your audience members confidently. You should stand up straight and walk toward the center of the speaking area with your head held high. As you take one purposeful step after another, remind yourself that you "have what it takes" and that you are "going to knock the audience's socks off." When you reach the center of the speaking area, turn and face your audience members, plant both of your feet firmly on the ground, and square your shoulders.

You are now ready for the second step—acknowledgment. Scan the audience from left to right, make eye contact with the people directly in front of you, and smile broadly and warmly. When you acknowledge your audience members, you are implicitly saying, "I see you, and you are important to me."

Now it is time for the third step—acceptance. You can accept your audience members by nodding slightly at the people directly in front of you as if to say, "Thank you for your willingness to listen to me." When you nod at your audience members, you are accepting your responsibility to say something important.

Finally, you should say "Good morning/afternoon/evening" in a strong, confident voice. Then pause briefly before delivering the opening line of your speech.

Notice that you should not utter a single word until after you have approached, acknowledged, and accepted your audience members. Don't make the mistake of starting your speech while you are walking to the center of the speaking area. Wait until you plant both feet on the ground, and you feel ready to begin. As I often tell my students, make your audience wait on you.

In summary, you should (1) approach your audience members confidently; (2) acknowledge your audience members; (3) accept your audience members; and (4) say "Good morning/afternoon/evening." This process may seem simple, but it really will make a powerful impact on your listeners. Get into the habit of greeting your audience before *every* speech so that you can significantly enhance your credibility.

Creating a Strong Bond

Once you begin speaking, your goal is to build a strong connection with your audience members by showing them that you care about their goals and their needs. You don't want your audience members to view you as a salesperson pitching a product. You want them to see you as a leader who has their best interests at heart.

According to Nick Morgan, you can strengthen your bond with your audience members by making your speech about them:

> Speakers find joy in public speaking when they realize that a speech is all about the audience, not the speaker ... These words are simple to say, but difficult to realize. Most speakers are so caught up in their own concerns and so driven to cover certain points or get a certain message across that they can't be bothered to think in more than a perfunctory way about the audience. And the irony is, of course, that there is no hope of getting your message across if that's all the energy you put into the audience ... So let go, and give the moment to the audience.[9]

Indeed, your objective is to make your speech "all about the audience." You can show your audience members that you care about them by using inclusive words, referencing the present, and highlighting the relevance.

One of the easiest ways to build a strong bond with your audience is to use inclusive words like *we* and *our* instead of *you* and *your*. As Shel Leanne points out, these words help "to send the message that the speaker and those listening are on the same team, in the same boat, facing the same fate."[10]

President George W. Bush demonstrated the value of using inclusive language when he spoke to the American people about the devastating impact of Hurricane Katrina:

> In the life of this nation, we have often been reminded that nature is an awesome force and that all life is fragile. We are the heirs of men and women who lived through those first terrible winters at Jamestown and Plymouth, who rebuilt Chicago after a great fire, and San Francisco after a great earthquake, who reclaimed the prairie from the dust bowl of the 1930s.
>
> Every time, the people of this land have come back from fire, flood, and storm to build anew—and to build better than what we had before. Americans have never left our destiny to the whims of nature, and we will not start now.
>
> These trials have also reminded us that we are often stronger than we know with the help of grace and one another. They remind us of a hope beyond all pain and death—a God who welcomes the lost to a house not made with hands.
>
> And they remind us that we are tied together in this life, in this nation and that the despair of any touches us all.[11]

Notice that President Bush doesn't say, "*You* have often been reminded that nature is an awesome force and that all life is fragile" or "*You* have never left your destiny to the whims of nature, and *you* will not start now." Instead, he uses the words *we*, *our*, and *us* to show his audience members that he is personally vested in the rebuilding process and that he shares their sorrow and their resolve.

There is a big difference between saying, "*You* must solve this problem" and "*We* must solve this problem." Whereas the first statement makes the audience responsible for solving the problem, the second statement implies that the speaker will work *with* the audience to solve the problem.

Don't tell your audience members what they should do. Use inclusive words to talk about what you and your audience members will accomplish together.

Referencing the Present

Another way to build a strong connection with your audience members is to reference the present. Although your listeners may think about their past and their future while you are speaking, they will spend most of their "thinking time" applying your ideas to their present needs and challenges. Think back to the information that you gathered during your audience analysis to determine the issues that your audience members are currently facing, and find ways to address those issues during your speech.

For instance, let's say that you are a middle manager who has overheard some of your direct reports discussing rumors of impending layoffs. Even though you have scheduled a meeting to discuss customer feedback, you could strengthen your bond with your employees by referencing the present:

> I recognize that it's difficult to stay focused when you've heard rumors about possible layoffs. But it's really important right now that we work hard to take care of our customers. I truly believe in each and every one of you, and I know that we have what it takes to help this company succeed.

You wouldn't want to start talking about customer feedback right away since your employees are clearly worried about losing their jobs. Although you may not be able to address the rumors directly, your employees will appreciate the fact that you understand how difficult it is for them "to stay focused." By referencing the present, you could show your employees that you understand how they feel and that you care about them.

You also can use this technique to enhance your credibility when you are speaking to a group of people that you don't know very well. Imagine that you are invited to offer career planning advice to a group of college seniors who are worried about their upcoming final exams. What could you say to make them listen to you? Here is one possibility:

> I know that you're all looking forward to getting your finals out of the way so you can hang out with your friends and enjoy your winter break. I was a college student not too long ago. I know how it is. But I hope that we can talk for just a few minutes about one simple question: "What's next?" Today, I want to help you think about what you will do after you earn your degree.

Your audience members would find this introduction appealing because it connects the topic of your speech (career planning) to their current primary concern (making it through final exams). While they might not initially want to think about their post-college plans, they will be more apt to listen to you once you tell them that you were "a college student not too long ago" and that you "know how it is."

Whether you know your audience well or not, make sure to reference the present near the beginning of your speech. Using this technique will show your audience members that you understand the issues they are facing right now.

Highlighting the Relevance

A simple technique that you can use to create a strong bond with your audience is to highlight the relevance of your speech. In other words, you want to show your audience members how your speech benefits *them*.

According to Nick Morgan, speakers must keep their audience members' needs at the forefront of their minds:

> To give them their due, most speakers are eager to communicate with their audiences. Unfortunately, that's where the good news ends. Most of them think "communication" means "telling them all you know." Preferably in list form ...
>
> We're an *audience*. That means we're always asking a very seminal question: *What's in it for me?* We never asked the speaker to tell us all he knows. We never asked the speaker to give us a list of the 15 most important things she cares about. We asked, *what's in it for me?*
>
> Audiences begin speeches asking "why"—why should I care, why is this important, why are you speaking and not me, why should I listen to you, and so on. If the speaker is successful—and it's a million to one shot against—the audience will end up asking "how"—how do I implement this idea, how do I make this my own, how do I get started, and so on.
>
> That's the speaker's job: take the audience from "why" to "how." But you can only do it by keeping that question—*what's in it for me?*—uppermost in your mind.[12]

Let's say that you are speaking to a group of colleagues about volunteering at a local homeless shelter. Everyone knows that helping the homeless is important. Nevertheless, you are more likely to make your message resonate if you tell your audience members why they should consider your idea:

> I want to invite all of you to join me at the homeless shelter tomorrow at 11 A.M. to prepare lunch for some of the homeless people in our community. This is a perfect opportunity for all of us to get to know one another better and spend a

few hours doing something that will make us feel really good about ourselves. I'm pretty sure that we'll laugh a lot as we figure out how to run the kitchen!

This example highlights the relevance of volunteering at the local homeless shelter by mentioning specific "benefits." It focuses on what audience members will get out of participating: the opportunity to "get to know one another better," "feel really good about ourselves," and "laugh a lot." Many audience members will find this appeal more compelling than one that merely focuses on how their participation will make a difference in the lives of others.

Think about the information that you gathered from your audience analysis whenever you are trying to figure out why your audience should care about what you are saying. This information can help you decide which "benefits" your audience members will find most compelling.

(handwritten at top) • narrow distance between you + audience physically + mentally

Owning the Room

(handwritten notes)
- own everywhere in room
- Keep audience in mind
- get to know on personal level
- remove physical barriers
- walk up + down isle, left + right make entire room your stage
- simple gesture eye contact

Powerful public speakers don't confine themselves to the area behind a lectern or a table. They own the room, not just the speaking area, by physically narrowing the distance between themselves and their audience.

Your opportunity to own the room begins once you know where you will be speaking. According to Gail Larsen, you should keep your audience in mind when you are deciding how the room will be set up:

> The way you set up your space will either support or diminish your capacity to be a transformational speaker. Ask your host to describe the room, the size and height of the stage or platform (or riser) if there is one, and the planned seating arrangements. If the venue does not provide the best environment for the experience you wish to create for your audience, ask for what you need. If adjustments are not forthcoming, consider how you yourself can alter the space, and arrive early enough to do so.[13]

Your objective is to make your audience members feel as if they can access you and get to know you on a personal level. If the stage seems too far away from the seats, move the seats forward. If there is a large table in front of the speaking area, push it off to the side. As Carmine Gallo explains, you don't want to "let anything come between you and your listeners … Think openness. Remove physical barriers—podiums, computers, chairs. Even a folder on a desk can break the connection and create distance."[14]

Another way to create a feeling of openness is to approach your audience members while you are speaking. If you are speaking in a large room, walk up and down the center aisle at least once. If you are speaking in a small room, walk toward the people on the far left side and the far right side a few different times so that they feel important. Don't deliver your entire speech from the center of the speaking area; make the entire room your stage.

When you approach your audience, select one specific person who is sitting nearby, and speak directly to her. Just focus on her for a few seconds, and ignore everyone else who is in the room. Make direct eye contact and smile. Show her that you care. Repeat this exercise with a few different people before walking back to the center of the speaking area. This simple gesture will show your audience members that you care about them individually, even if you haven't yet had the opportunity to meet them.

Remember to own the room every time you speak. Don't let the room setup dictate where you should sit or stand. Make the room yours so that you can narrow the distance between you and your audience members.

Discussion Questions

1. How do you conduct an audience analysis?
2. What does it mean to take your audience members on a "first date"?
3. How can you project authority?
4. What is the benefit of having someone introduce you?
5. What is the proper way to greet your audience?
6. How can you show your audience members that you care about their needs?
7. Why is it important to use inclusive words?
8. How does referencing the present enhance your credibility?
9. Why is it important to highlight the relevance of your speech?
10. How can you "own the room"?

PART 3

USING YOUR VOICE

The Music of Speech

Powerful public speakers rely on two distinct, but complementary components to deliver a message—words and music. They select the words that will help them express an idea, and then they "coat" these words with music to convey a particular meaning.[1]

According to Heifetz and Linsky, speakers often use the musical properties of speech to express how they feel:

> In small ways, we do this every day. For example, if you ask someone how he is doing, and he says "OK," you can hear a big difference between a bright accent on the "K" and a sad emphasis on the "O."[2]

Indeed, humans have the unique ability to share their emotions using a vocal structure that is remarkably efficient at creating complex sounds. The position of the larynx (where the vocal cords are located) is low in the neck, enabling a high degree of sound modification. As Jean Gregg notes, the "vocal fold is adjustable in length, tension, and shape, giving the human larynx top honors for vocal versatility."[3] Given this degree of versatility, humans are able to use their voice to express themselves in unique and powerful ways.

The renowned composer, Leonard Bernstein, asserts that "music does possess the power of expressivity, and the human being does innately possess the capacity to respond to it."[4] In other words, music isn't simply a group of sounds; it is a communication device that has a specific, quantifiable role in speech. Music "sounds the way feelings feel" and "can express the forms of vital experience which language [alone] is peculiarly unfit to convey."[5]

For this reason, speakers should leverage the music of their voice to enhance their verbal message. Although words alone can be powerful, the perfect combination of music and language can create unparalleled impact. "As a tool for activation of specific thoughts, music is not as good as language. As a tool for arousing feelings and emotions, music is better than language. The combination of the two … is the best."[6]

Your goal as a speaker is to leverage the music of your voice to enhance your verbal message. But before you can create a powerful symphony of words, you must warm up your instrument.

Tuning Your Voice

L ike any instrument, your voice is not always ready to produce the highest quality sound. Think about what you sound like when you first wake up in the morning. You certainly wouldn't want to sound this way when you speak to your audience!

Given that your audience members will form an impression of you within a matter of seconds, it is important that you do everything you can to open powerfully. Don't make the mistake of clearing your voice or coughing before you begin your speech. Instead, remember to tune your voice before your speech so you're able to get off to a strong start.

Singing Musical Scales

One of the simplest ways to tune your voice is to sing musical scales—groups of notes arranged in ascending or descending order.

Have you ever heard the catchy tune "Do-Re-Mi" from *The Sound of Music*? Music teachers all over the world use a variation of this tune to help their students learn how to sing. The full tune is actually a major scale made up of different syllables, each sung at a particular pitch. The syllables are Do, Re, Mi, Fa, Sol, La, Ti, Do. (Musical scales are made up of seven notes; the eighth note is the same as the first note, except in a higher octave.)

Try singing the major scale to tune your voice. Go ahead. Stand up, relax your shoulders, breathe in, and sing "Dooooooo." Hold the note for two seconds before stopping. Now sing "Reeeeeee" at a slightly higher pitch. Repeat this process until you sing all eight notes. Let's start again from the top. "Dooooooo-Reeeeeee-Miiiiiii-Faaaaaaa-Sollllllll-Laaaaaaa-Tiiiiiii-Dooooooo."

The next step is to begin with the final "Do" and work your way down the musical scale, lowering your pitch ever so slightly between notes. Ready? Relax your shoulders, breathe in, and sing: "Dooooooo-Tiiiiiii-Laaaaaaa-Sollllllll-Faaaaaaa-Miiiiiii-Reeeeeee-Dooooooo."

Now repeat the process one more time. Work your way up the musical scale and then down the musical scale.

Although this exercise may seem silly, it really will help you speak powerfully. Make sure to sing musical scales before every speech so that your voice will be warmed up when you are ready to begin.

Producing Powerful Sounds

Another way to tune your voice is to practice producing powerful sounds. The objective is to train yourself to take in enough air so that you don't sound lackluster or trail off at the ends of sentences.

The best way to learn how to produce powerful sounds is to practice taking in as much air as you can and then releasing the air as you say the word "power."

Let's give this exercise a try. Stand up and relax your shoulders. Now take a deep breath in through your mouth. Don't breathe in through your nose. Open your mouth and fill up your lungs with air. When you feel like your lungs are completely full, say the word "power" as though you are throwing the word against the wall in front of you.

Now try the exercise again. This time, try to take in even more air and remind yourself that you are a leader as you release the word "power." You want to ensure that you throw the word, not just say it. Release the word loudly and sharply; make the "p" in "power" sound like an explosion.

This exercise is designed to help you strengthen your voice and reinforce your leadership mindset. If you take this exercise seriously, you will be able to speak in a firmer, more confident voice that your audience will perceive as credible and authoritative.

Five Key Musical Elements

N ow that you know how to tune your voice, it is time to examine the building blocks that you will use to "coat" your words with emotion—the five key musical elements.

When composers create a piece of music, they use precise combinations of musical elements to elicit specific emotional responses. Powerful public speakers leverage these elements in the same way to shape the "music" of their message. For example, Martin Luther King Jr. used the five key musical elements to transform his "I Have a Dream" speech into a moving song. Without these elements, King's delivery would have been far less dramatic.

Composers often use five key musical elements to craft memorable pieces of music: tempo, dynamics, pitch, timbre, and rhythm. Although composers leverage other musical elements as well, these five elements are especially useful in public speeches.

You may not be familiar with these musical elements if you don't play an instrument or sing in a chorus. But don't worry. After you explore the music and speech examples in the following sections, you will be able to describe these elements in specific and meaningful ways.

Tempo

The tempo is the general speed of the sound. You can characterize tempo by asking yourself:

- Does the music have a fast, frenetic pace, or is it very slow?
- Does the pulse change suddenly?
- Does the speed fluctuate a lot?

Fast tempos typically generate excitement, energy, and action, while slow tempos often elicit reflection and solemnity. For example, Nikolai Rimsky-Korsakov's *Flight of the Bumblebee* speeds along at a breakneck pace to capture the frenetic motions of a berserk insect. In contrast, Richard Strauss' *Death and Transfiguration* crawls along at a lethargic pace to transport listeners to a room housing a man on his deathbed.

Choosing a fast or slow tempo is not the only way to leverage this particular element; tempo contrasts are also vital. In his 1988 address at the Democratic National Convention, Jesse Jackson varies the tempo of his speech to convey his strong belief in equality for all Americans. Jackson begins by presenting the state of racial discrimination in America at a moderately slow pace. But soon he begins to increase his tempo to express a passionate desire for racial equality. Jackson's quickening tempo helps reinforce the urgency of creating a better tomorrow.[7]

The main reason that Jackson starts slowly is to give his audience members a chance to adjust to his speaking style. As Jeanette and Roy Henderson confirm, this initial "slowness" really matters:

> These moments should be considered as a kind of "settling in" of your voice, just like settling into a comfortable old armchair. It takes a minute to get all the right parts of the body in all of the right places, just as it takes [time for an audience] to settle in and get comfortable with your voice.[8]

The next time you deliver a speech, start slowly. Once your audience members are accustomed to your voice, you can vary the tempo of your speech to keep them engaged.

Dynamics

Dynamics is a musical term for volume. You can characterize dynamics by asking yourself:

- Is the volume always loud or always soft?
- Does the volume suddenly become loud and then suddenly soft?
- Is the change in volume very gradual?

Although there are no universal rules, loud sounds tend to be startling, alarming, and grand, whereas soft sounds tend to be sad, brooding, and ominous. For instance, Modest Mussorgsky's *Night on Bald Mountain* produces a turbulent seaside mountain image. The piece opens with a rise in volume and then a sudden fall in volume, which produces a heaving sensation as if waves are washing ashore in a violent fashion before receding and rising again.

Indeed, dynamics dramatically influence an audience's mood and excitement level. Speakers can use dynamics to excite or surprise, but they also can use dynamics to soothe and calm. President Bill Clinton illustrates the use of dynamics to assuage an audience in his 1995 address in Oklahoma City four days after the bombing. At the beginning of each sentence, President Clinton's voice is strong and appropriately loud. As each sentence concludes, his voice quiets and tapers downward. By effectively using dynamics, President Clinton conveys the need to move from thoughts of anger and hatred to thoughts of acceptance and unity.[9]

It is important to keep the occasion in mind as you deliver your speech so that you speak at the appropriate volume. You wouldn't want to belt out a eulogy at a funeral. You would want to speak softly and calmly to match the somberness of the occasion. Similarly, you wouldn't want to whisper a toast at a wedding reception. You would want to speak loudly and energetically as you share anecdotes about the newlyweds.

Pitch

Pitch refers to how low or high a note is and where the note is located in the musical scale. Singers are categorized based on the pitch of their voice. Men are often classified into vocal categories such as bass, baritone, and tenor, while women are classified into vocal categories such as alto and soprano. You can characterize pitch by asking yourself:

- Is the sound high-pitched like a typical female voice or bird, or is it low-pitched like a typical male voice or lion?
- Are there very high and very low notes?
- Do pitches change gradually in small steps as in a musical scale, or do they wildly jump up and down in large intervals?

High pitches tend to be energizing and exciting, while low pitches tend to be dark and morose. In *November Woods*, for instance, Arnold Bax purposefully alternates between low and high pitched notes to create a sense of unpredictable motion. Bax leverages pitch to transport his listeners to a mysterious world of rustling leaves and howling winds.

Mohandas Gandhi, in his 1931 address at Kingsley Hall, focuses on pitch for a different reason: to emphasize his firm belief in a higher power. Gandhi generally maintains a constant tempo and speaks in a blunt, steady voice that lacks any semblance of pride or passion. The most noticeable change occurs as he modulates the pitch of his voice. Had Gandhi not altered his pitch from phrase to phrase, his speech would have been bland and robotic; by varying just pitch, he effectively conveys his resolve and reverence.[10]

The lesson here is that you can use different pitches to convey distinct emotions. According to Dan O'Hair, Hannah Rubenstein, and Rob Stewart, the pitch of your voice "conveys your mood, reveals your level of enthusiasm, expresses your concern for the audience, and signals your overall commitment to the occasion."[11] Don't limit yourself to the typical range of your voice. Allow yourself to express intensity, seriousness, and happiness by varying your pitch.

Timbre

Timbre (pronounced tam-ber) is the "character" or "personality" of a specific sound. You can tell the difference between your mother's voice and your father's voice because each voice has a distinct timbre. You can characterize timbre by asking yourself:

- Is the sound rough, biting, sweet, warm, obtrusive, or sonorous?
- Are certain notes heavily emphasized or accented more than others?
- Is there a sharp and alarming emphasis at the beginning of the note, or is there a more subtle and dull emphasis throughout the note's duration?

Think of timbre in terms of the various sounds produced by different musical instruments. In *November Woods*, Arnold Bax creates suspense, magic, and restlessness by using the harp, high strings, and flutes, which feature thin, airy, ethereal, and rustling timbres. Conversely, Richard Strauss reinforces a morose and resigned atmosphere in *Death and Transfiguration* by using "sad" sounding instruments such as the bassoon and oboe.

In her 1992 address at the Democratic National Convention, Elizabeth Glaser takes advantage of the natural timbre of her voice to deliver an emotional message about the AIDS crisis. Glaser uses a natural and noticeable timbre to evoke a variety of emotional responses. She adjusts her timbre to convey anger when discussing the lack of government action and convey hopefulness when highlighting the possibility of real change. Glaser's vocal timbre is firm and deliberate—as is her conviction.[12]

As this example illustrates, you can leverage the natural timbre of your voice to convey powerful emotions. While you can't change the general quality of your voice, you can use your own distinctive timbre to emphasize certain themes and ideas.

Rhythm

Rhythm is the structural spacing of the sounds. Different combinations of notes and pauses create very different rhythms. You can characterize rhythm by asking yourself:

- Do the sounds occur in regular and constant time intervals, or is there significant variation and unpredictability among the sounds?
- Do pauses occur suddenly after a flourish of notes, or do the notes slowly ease into a natural break?
- Are the pauses of significant duration, or are they more like short breaths?

Composers use variations in rhythm to achieve their musical objectives. Gustav Holst's *Mars* (from *The Planets*) presents a regimented and steady rhythm repeated ad nauseam that enables listeners to visualize an army of soldiers marching in strict time. On the other hand, Aaron Copland's *Gun Battle* (from *Billy the Kid*) uses pauses of varying lengths, as well as quick irregular rhythmic flurries, to produce an unpredictable but exciting atmosphere that keeps listeners alert and on edge.

Although every speaker naturally employs some rhythmic technique, Tom Hanks carefully manages his rhythm in his 2005 commencement address at Vassar College to deliver a powerful, engaging message. Hanks' ever-changing rhythmic pattern forces listeners to hang on to each phrase and wait in anticipation for the next one. When he introduces a key idea—such as the simplicity of removing four cars from the road to eliminate gridlock—he uses pauses of varying lengths to emphasize the importance of what he is saying.[13]

Hanks' speech underscores the power of pausing. As Jeanette and Roy Henderson remind us, "a moment of intentional, active silence creates the most dynamic, deliberate reaction you could ever hope to achieve."[14] With a simple pause, you can redirect attention, create anticipation, or defuse a tense situation.

Layering Musical Elements

Powerful public speakers combine, or layer, the five key musical elements to convey a variety of emotions. The human voice is a dynamic instrument capable of evoking every possible sentiment, and speakers throughout history have harnessed the music of their voice to transmit distinct and enduring messages. In their own unique ways, powerful public speakers have leveraged musical elements to achieve a variety of objectives, such as inciting political change, calming public outrage, or inspiring a generation.

If you want to become a powerful public speaker, you must think like a composer who is creating a piece of music. Your objective is to layer the five key musical elements on top of one another to state and restate themes, evoke emotion, and build to a climax.[15]

Stating and Restating Themes

The first step to creating a musical masterpiece is to decide on a theme. The theme of a composition is typically a recognizable melody that shapes the rest of the piece.[16] Often, a composer will start with a simple one-line melody or a melody with an accompaniment, and build the rest of the piece around that theme. For example, Ludwig van Beethoven's famous Symphony No. 5 is based on four notes. These four notes present a "fate knocking on the door" motif that is revisited throughout the piece in a variety of ways. As James Humes articulates in *Speak Like Churchill, Stand Like Lincoln*, compositions like Beethoven's Symphony No. 5 "may have [multiple] movements, but [always will] have one dominant melody."[17]

In her 1995 remarks to the United Nations 4th World Conference on Women, Hillary Clinton uses several compelling techniques to underscore her primary theme—protecting and respecting women's rights. Clinton emphasizes the importance of human rights for women through the rhythmic repetition of the phrase, "It is a violation of human rights," but she also raises her pitch when she says the word "human" to draw attention to her theme that "human rights are women's rights." Clinton's blatant, almost staccato delivery makes her message even more meaningful as she explains that these issues must be heard "loudly" and "clearly" and that "we must move beyond rhetoric."[18]

You can deliver an equally powerful speech if you focus on the main message that you want to convey. Identify your primary theme—your one big idea—and repeat it over and over again in emotionally evocative ways.

Evoking Emotion

One of the reasons music evokes powerful emotions is that it mirrors the "main characteristics of emotional behavior, speech, and thought."[19] In other words, different musical "settings" elicit specific types of feelings: a medium tempo, loud, and concordant arrangement is more likely to evoke happiness than a slow, muted, and slightly discordant one.[20] For instance, Elmer Bernstein's *The Magnificent Seven* begins at a comfortable pace, with loud and assertive proclamations from the full orchestra, before launching into a galloping theme that evokes adventure and excitement. In contrast, Gustav Holst's *Mars* (from *The Planets*) features low-pitched brass instruments with a deep, dark drone that create an ominous image and evoke fear and alarm.

Mario Savio, an American political activist, leverages certain tempo, volume, and rhythm "settings" in his 1964 sit-in address at the steps of

Sproul Hall at the University of California, Berkeley to motivate his audience members to fight for free speech. Savio speaks about the power of nonviolent civil disobedience with a tensile rapidity, without dramatic pauses or thought breaks. The panting Savio speaks quickly and assertively to generate excitement and inspire his listeners to "put [their] bodies upon the gears and upon the wheels, upon the levers, upon all the apparatus ... to make [the machine] stop!" Savio's use of musical elements enables him to harness the energy of a crowd calling for change.[21]

Think of the five key musical elements as levers that you can pull to create the desired musical "settings." You can drop your pitch to emphasize a point, speed up your tempo to produce a sense of urgency, or increase your volume to generate excitement. Spend time "coating" certain phrases with the appropriate music so that you can make your audience members feel the same way you do.

Building to a Climax

Every piece of music must reach a climax and a subsequent resolution. Without these elements, the audience may leave without a clear sense of the composer's primary message. As a result, composers often use a crescendo to signal to musicians that they should gradually increase the volume of their instruments. There are two ways that musicians create this effect: "one in which the tone increases in power while it is being sounded and another in which succeeding tones are each sounded louder than the preceding one."[22] For example, Gustav Mahler's Symphony No. 5 closes with a jubilant chorale that includes crescendos during the sustained notes. Following the chorale, the strings and woodwinds dramatically increase their tempo, while slowly increasing their volume with each successive flourish up and down the registers of their instruments.

In his 2009 address to a Joint Session of Congress, President Barack Obama champions the importance of passing health care reform legislation. He speaks with conviction about the "character of our country" and raises the volume of his voice as he explains that the "politically safe move would be to kick the can further down the road—to defer reform one more year, or one more election, or one more term." With each successive line, his voice grows louder and louder and his tempo quickens until he reaches the climax of his speech: "I still believe we can do great things, and that here and now we will meet history's test. Because that's who we are, that is our calling, *that* is our character."[23]

You will be able to end your speech with conviction and power, just like President Obama, if you use a crescendo to make your audience members feel as though they are climbing to the peak of a mountain. A well-placed crescendo will help you heighten anticipation, create momentum, and leave a lasting impression.

Discussion Questions

1. What is the "music of speech"?
2. Why is the human voice remarkably efficient at producing complex sounds?
3. Why is it important to tune your voice before you begin speaking?
4. What are musical scales?
5. How can you practice producing powerful sounds?
6. What are the five key musical elements?
7. What does it mean to "layer" musical elements?
8. How can you weave your theme throughout your speech?
9. How can you use musical elements to evoke emotion?
10. Why should you use a crescendo at the end of your speech?

PART 4

CONSTRUCTING MEMORABLE MESSAGES

Powerful Language

T he foundation of every memorable message is powerful language—combinations of words that take an audience on an emotional journey.

You can't expect to stir your audience by repeating the first words that pop into your head. You will only move your audience members if you think carefully about where you are going, and then choose words that will help you take them there.

As Keith and Lundberg explain, you must carefully select the words that you use to communicate your ideas:

> Think of it this way: you don't go out of the house naked, but you choose what to wear. Well, your ideas don't just leave your head "naked" by themselves, but you choose words for them. Like your wardrobe, you have a choice about the words you use. They can be plain or fancy, cheap or expensive, sexy or boring; they can show off your deepest thoughts or hide them. Just as there is no neutral way to dress (after all, anything you put on is a choice that says something about you), there is no neutral way of choosing words when speaking.[1]

Indeed, your challenge is to find a "wardrobe" for your message that will make your audience members want to listen to you. Two ways to enhance your language wardrobe are to use imagery and symbolism.

Imagery

Determining which words to use is an essential part of crafting a compelling message. However, words alone are not memorable. What your audience members will remember are the *images* that you use to describe people and places, colors and textures, sounds and smells.

According to Jeanette and Roy Henderson, it is important to think of speeches as arrangements of images, not as arrangements of words:

> Consider each individual image you create as a single brick, which, when placed next to other bricks, will soon become a row. Then you begin another row on top of that one, and another, until eventually, every row contributes to the completion of the wall, which is your entire presentation.[2]

Powerful public speakers don't just talk about a cause that matters to them; they use imagery to *show* the audience that they care. Shel Leanne reminds us that "words filled with descriptive power can deepen the impact of speech. Drawing on richly descriptive words can create multilayered communication that enables a speaker to make great strides toward articulating their vision with great efficacy."[3]

By delivering powerful images, you narrow the distance between you and your listeners; you enable your listeners to think your thoughts and feel your feelings. You put your listeners in your shoes and enable them to take the same steps that you have taken. Once your listeners are in your shoes, they are more likely to believe what you believe and do what you want them to do.

President Barack Obama masterfully demonstrated how to use powerful images during his now famous 2004 Democratic National Convention speech:

> I'm not talking about blind optimism here—the almost willful ignorance that thinks unemployment will go away if we just don't think about it, or the health care crisis will solve

itself if we just ignore it. That's not what I'm talking about. I'm talking about something more substantial. It's the hope of slaves sitting around a fire singing freedom songs; the hope of immigrants setting out for distant shores; the hope of a young naval lieutenant bravely patrolling the Mekong Delta; the hope of a millworker's son who dares to defy the odds; the hope of a skinny kid with a funny name who believes that America has a place for him, too.[4]

President Obama uses vivid imagery to enable his listeners to hear the slaves singing freedom songs and feel the fear of a young officer on patrol. He paints pictures of places such as "distant shores" and the Mekong Delta and paints pictures of people such as slaves and immigrants. President Obama even creates a striking, somewhat self-deprecating portrait of himself by using adjectives like "skinny" and "funny" to elicit awkwardness that nearly everyone can identify with. Through his use of imagery, President Obama conveys the power of hope and inspires his audience to join the movement for change.

Like President Obama, you can use powerful images to set your message in motion and make it stick in the minds of your listeners. By using highly descriptive words, you will be able to make your audience members feel like they are standing next to you and experiencing the same moment that you are experiencing.

Symbolism

A technique closely related to creating images is leveraging symbols. Like images, symbols evoke specific ideas and emotions. However, symbols often suggest deeper meanings.

I frequently use an exercise called "Step on Mom" to help my students understand the power of symbols.[5] I ask the students to write down the name of a food that they hate on one slip of paper, the name of an insect that they fear on another slip of paper, and the name of a person that they love on a third slip of paper. Then I tell them to step on the three pieces of paper—one at a time. The students have no trouble stepping on the first two slips of paper, but they usually abstain from stepping on the third slip of paper.

I often ask, "Why are you having such a tough time stepping on the third slip of paper? You're only stepping on a word." Inevitably, at least one student will respond, "No, I'm stepping on what that word represents—the love that I feel for my mother." The lesson, of course, is that words have symbolic meaning.

Symbols are useful devices that can help you express ideas and emotions that you may not want to explicitly share, but that you feel are important for your audience members to understand. For example, you could invoke the Berlin Wall, a defining symbol of the Cold War, to discuss a contentious issue that is creating a divide or barrier within your organization.

You also can use symbols to discuss intangible concepts such as hope, love, or change. For instance, you could talk about the American flag to evoke feelings of patriotism and pride or talk about a dove to convey the importance of peace and hope.

Don't shy away from exploring difficult or abstract concepts. Use symbols to make your message even more meaningful.

Anecdotes

One of the most effective ways to captivate an audience is to tell a story. Powerful stories make people think about who they are, what they believe, and whether what they are doing is right.

Although many individuals use the terms "story" and "anecdote" interchangeably, these terms have distinct meanings. Stories are typically longer, detailed narratives, while anecdotes are shorter, descriptive vignettes. This distinction helps explain why we often struggle to tell compelling stories within the framework of a speech. Many speakers find themselves conveying stories that are either too long or too complex and as a result, often notice their listeners taking short, unplanned naps. It is not that these speakers are uninteresting or uncreative. They simply need to learn how to construct memorable *anecdotes* instead of long, complex stories.

The key to telling a powerful anecdote is to create a *moment*—a snapshot in time that engages listeners in an emotional experience. Think of a moment as a single photograph within a frame. Whenever powerful public speakers share an anecdote, they verbally recreate the particular photograph that they are envisioning. These speakers force themselves to stay within the frame so that their anecdote is succinct and meaningful. In other words, they don't describe what they "see" outside the periphery; they only talk about what they "see" in the photograph.

Each individual anecdote within a speech should be no more than a minute long. Remember: You don't need to share every detail with your audience. You simply need to describe what is happening in the particular photograph that you are holding in your mind.

Every powerful anecdote is made up of four interconnected elements: the setting, the characters, the plot, and the moral. Let's explore these elements one at a time.

Setting

The first element of an anecdote is the setting. Many speakers think of the setting as the backdrop of the anecdote—the time and place where the anecdote occurs. More appropriately, the setting is the time and place where you want to take your listeners.

You can transport your listeners to any moment in the past, the present, or the future, as long as you help them visualize the place that you are taking them. If your backdrop is a hospital, for instance, tell your audience members exactly where the situation occurred—the waiting room, the doctor's office, or the main hallway—and then use details to help them "walk there" in their minds.

Consider the following example:

> We had arrived at our destination—a large waiting room containing a few dusty chairs caked in a thick layer of grey dust, a round wood veneer table masked with dozens of tattered, discolored *Physician's Digest* magazines and a broken etch-a-sketch depicting a partially completed game of tic-tac-toe.[6]

Notice that the speaker uses the term "large waiting room" instead of "hospital" to illuminate the backdrop and then fills in the picture using powerful details like "a round wood veneer table," "dozens of tattered, discolored *Physician's Digest* magazines," and "a broken etch-a-sketch depicting a partially completed game of tic-tac-toe." In doing so, the speaker effectively transports his listeners to the waiting room in his anecdote.

Whenever you introduce a setting, use details to paint a clear picture of the environment that you are describing. You want to make it as easy as possible for your audience members to "walk there" in their minds.

Characters

The characters in your anecdote animate your setting. They are the individuals through whom your audience members envision a specific situation.

Your anecdote should only have one or two main characters. By limiting the number of characters in your anecdote, you will make it easier for your audience members to get to know them.

Marshall Ganz explains that an anecdote will only "work" if your audience members can emotionally identify with the main characters:

> Through our empathetic identification with a protagonist, we experience the emotional content ... what [the anecdote] has to teach to our hearts, not only our heads ... Arguments persuade with evidence, logic, and data. [Short] stories persuade by this empathetic identification.[7]

Your audience members will "fall into" your anecdote if they can see some part of themselves or someone they know in the characters. Consequently, you should introduce the characters at a high-level, and then provide the "mental space" for listeners to fill in the details themselves.

Consider this description of a character named Jasmine:

> As we headed toward the exit, a playful young girl ran over, threw her hands in the air and exclaimed, "Pick me up!" Her name was Jasmine. She was an elementary school student who was quite tall for her age. Her almond shaped eyes seemed to cover most of her lightly freckled face. Jasmine

wore a large bright smile with one strategically absent lower front tooth.[8]

In this example, the speaker introduces us to a character named Jasmine. He tells us that Jasmine is an energetic elementary school student who has "almond shaped eyes," a "lightly freckled face," and a "strategically absent lower front tooth." However, he doesn't specify Jasmine's age, race, height, eye color, or hair color. As a result, each of us can envision Jasmine as someone much like ourselves or someone we know.

The next time you are developing characters, think of Jasmine. Remember to introduce your characters in ways that enable your audience members to envision them and identify with them.

Plot

The plot is the action sequence—the events that take place within the photograph. In other words, the plot is a short synopsis of a moment in time.

According to Ganz, a powerful plot consists of three components: a challenge, a choice, and an outcome. These components form the basis of a memorable and engaging narrative:

> As the plot begins (once upon a time), our protagonist is going along her way to a desired goal. But what happens? All of a sudden something stops her in her tracks. She didn't plan for this ... Will it turn out all right? Will she succeed or fail? As her efforts unfold, the suspense builds to a climax when things are resolved by getting back on the old track, getting on a new track to the old goal, or getting on a new track to a new goal. There is a resolution.[9]

Although there are many different types of plots, the most powerful plots focus on inflection points—critical moments in our lives that have important long-term implications. These moments are challenging because they force us to examine our beliefs, our priorities, and our values. Plots that explore inflection points take us on a meaningful journey through our own lives and engage our hearts and minds in a very personal way.

Consider the following example:

I will never forget the gut-wrenching, panic infused nausea that paralyzed my body during the seconds leading up to the moment when the plastic hour hand of the clock struck five. For at that moment, my brother casually walked across the room and reached up towards the shiny red lever that was just within reach of his chubby right hand.

Moments later, dizzied by the flashing alarm lights and piercing screams from the fire alarm speaker, I stumbled through the office's door, down the dark hallway towards the glowing emergency exit sign. As my family and I rushed down the spiraling emergency stairway to evacuate the building, Dr. Andrews, who had had hurriedly left the office with us, turned to my parents and sternly said, "Greg is autistic and will require around the clock assistance for the rest of his life." Even though I didn't know what autism was at the time, the darkness of my parents' stare, void of all emotion, said it all. I knew at that moment that life would never be the same ...Why had this happened to my family?

From that day forward, each night I prayed—I pleaded that I would find some way to help Greg live life to its fullest. I searched day and night for a program that would enable my brother to build the self-confidence required to reach his true potential and live independently ...

If it wasn't for the LABBB Collaborative, a publicly-funded provider of educational programming and support services for Massachusetts autistic students, Dr. Andrews may have been right. However, through LABBB's specialized curriculum, my brother, as well as hundreds of other special need students from the surrounding area learned how to develop and build the real-life skills and social aptitudes necessary to function in society.[10]

The speaker connects with us emotionally by highlighting an inflection point in his life—the moment that Dr. Andrews turns to his parents and says, "Greg is autistic and will require around the clock assistance for the rest of his life." This is a moment with which we all can relate; after all, everyone knows someone who has dealt with a difficult diagnosis. The speaker engages our hearts and minds by clearly delineating the challenge (learning that his brother was autistic), the choice (committing to finding a program that would enable his brother to live independently), and the outcome (seeing his brother acquire the skills necessary to lead a normal life).

As this example illustrates, powerful plots highlight a challenge, a choice, and an outcome that make us think about our own experiences and how certain decisions have shaped our lives. These plots keep us engaged by taking us on a roller-coaster ride that stirs our emotions.

Moral

Powerful anecdotes don't just entertain us. They impart specific lessons that motivate us to change something about ourselves or the world around us:

> We tell [short] stories to make something happen, to achieve a response, to get a reaction, to have an effect ... We deploy them because we want to make a point ... They are not simply an example, an illustration, a case in point. When they are well told we experience the point—we feel hope, we feel relieved, we feel connected—and it is that experience, not the words as such, that can move us to action.[11]

Think back to elementary school when you heard the anecdote of the tortoise and the hare. When the tortoise dared the hare to a race, you expected the hare to win since he was much faster than the tortoise. However, you probably were surprised to learn that the tortoise actually won the race by crawling to the finish line while the hare took a nap. The moral, of course, is that perseverance pays off and that working at a slow and steady pace has its benefits.

The reason that you tell an anecdote in the first place is to share an important idea or life lesson with your audience members. As such, you must explain what they should take away from your anecdote. Don't expect them to know what you mean. Be clear about what the moral is and why it is valuable.

Repetition

The easiest way to make your message memorable is to repeat it over and over and over again. After all, the more often you say something, the more likely your audience members are to remember it.

Keith and Lundberg note that repetition will help make ordinary phrases much more memorable:

> Even though people commonly repeat many words in ordinary conversation, structured repetition is generally avoided. Yet in a speech, such repetition can add emphasis and make a point more memorable ... In other words, listeners will like repetition even if they don't know why.[12]

Although there are many different types of repetition techniques, powerful public speakers frequently use three techniques to emphasize certain ideas without sounding like a talking parrot: anaphora, epistrophe, and alliteration.

Anaphora

Anaphora is the repetition of a word or phrase at the beginning of successive clauses or sentences. It is used to draw attention to a specific idea.

Consider how Martin Luther King Jr. uses anaphora in his famous "I Have a Dream" speech:

> *I have a dream* that one day this nation will rise up and live out the true meaning of its creed: "We hold these truths to be self-evident, that all men are created equal."
>
> *I have a dream* that one day on the red hills of Georgia, the sons of former slaves and the sons of former slave owners will be able to sit down together at the table of brotherhood.
>
> *I have a dream* that one day even the state of Mississippi, a state sweltering with the heat of injustice, sweltering with the heat of oppression, will be transformed into an oasis of freedom and justice.
>
> *I have a dream* that my four little children will one day live in a nation where they will not be judged by the color of their skin but by the content of their character.
>
> *I have a dream* today![13]

King's repetition of the phrase "I have a dream" at the beginning of successive sentences emphasizes the power and majesty of his dream—"that one day this nation will rise up and live out the true meaning of its creed: 'We hold these truths to be self-evident, that all men are created equal.'"

President Barack Obama uses anaphora at the end of his 2008 Democratic National Convention speech to accentuate an equally powerful idea:

> America, we cannot turn back … *not with* so much work to be done; *not with* so many children to educate, and so many veterans to care for; *not with* an economy to fix, and cities to rebuild, and farms to save; *not with* so many families to protect and so many lives to mend.[14]

President Obama repeats the phrase "not with" at the beginning of successive clauses to underscore the large number of problems facing the American people. By using anaphora, he magnifies the importance of making progress.

Indeed, anaphora is a powerful rhetorical device that you can use to emphasize a key idea that you want your audience to remember.

Epistrophe

The opposite of anaphora is epistrophe, the repetition of a word or phrase at the end of successive clauses or sentences. Powerful public speakers use epistrophe in the same way that they do anaphora—to drive home a key idea.

Consider the following excerpt from President Lyndon Johnson's "We Shall Overcome" speech, which he delivered in 1965 amid racial violence in the South: "There is no Negro *problem*. There is no Southern *problem*. There is no Northern *problem*. There is only an American *problem*."[15]

President Johnson repeats the word "problem" at the end of successive sentences to emphasize that racial discrimination is a national problem that tests the strength of American democracy.

Like Johnson, you can leverage this device to emphasize a problem, but you can also use it to create a sense of urgency. Consider the following example:

> We may not be able to cure cancer tomorrow, but we can still take steps to fight this disease *today*. We can donate our time and our money *today*. We can urge our friends to get involved *today*. There's no time to wait.

The repetition of the word "today" at the end of successive sentences underscores the importance of acting right now.

As is the case with anaphora, you can use epistrophe nearly anywhere in a speech to highlight a key idea.

Alliteration

Alliteration is the repetition of consonant sounds of nearby words. It gives words a musical quality and makes them more memorable.

Have you ever noticed how easily "Krispy Kreme" and "Seattle Seahawks" roll off your tongue? The "kr" sound in Krispy Kreme and the "sea" sound in Seattle Seahawks make these names easy to remember and repeat.

Powerful public speakers use alliteration within a group of nearby words to create the same effect. For example, read the following sentence aloud: "Some modern women remember names." Doesn't it have a nice ring to it? The repeated "m" sound makes this sentence pleasing to hear.

President Ronald Reagan uses alliteration in his 1981 inaugural address to lay out his vision for the nation: "In the days ahead, I will propose *removing* the *roadblocks* that have slowed our economy and *reduced* productivity. Steps will be taken aimed at *restoring* the balance between the various levels of government."[16]

Notice that President Reagan uses four words that begin with the letter "r" when discussing his goals. The repeated "r" sound makes these goals sound more dynamic and more appealing.

Alliteration is a powerful rhetorical tool that you can use to make your key ideas stand out. Write down a few words with similar consonant sounds, and then try to link them together to form a single sentence.

Closing the Loop

One final way to craft a memorable message is to close the loop, or end where you started. You can leave a strong impression on your audience members by revisiting an idea or an anecdote that you introduced at the beginning of your speech.

Consider the following speech introduction:

> Six years ago, I probably would have guessed that only elderly people in poor health suffer strokes. I would have been wrong. At age 50, my father experienced a spontaneous dissection of his carotid artery—the rarest form of stroke—with no health-related cause. The bleeding swiftly encapsulated his brain, leaving my father paralyzed on the right side of his body and unable to speak all but a few words. The speech disorder, known as aphasia, not only affects his ability to process language, but also inhibits reading and writing …
>
> Over one million Americans struggle with aphasia. That's over twice as many people living with Parkinson's disease, cerebral palsy, or spinal cord injuries, yet there is little public awareness of aphasia's pervasiveness … It's time to give this silent disorder a voice and to let the people who we love and who are suffering with aphasia know that there is help available. Aphasia does not mean "alone." Aphasia does not mean "hopeless." Aphasia does not mean "silence."[17]

In this example, the speaker introduces her topic by discussing her father's struggle with aphasia. She starts to educate her audience about "aphasia's pervasiveness" and the need to "give this silent disorder a voice."

At the end of her speech, the speaker asks her audience members to wear a gray wristband to show their support for people living with aphasia. She makes a strong impact on her audience members by revisiting her father's journey:

> Maybe you wear the wristband in honor of my father, maybe you wear it in honor of your own family member, or maybe you wear it to speak on behalf of those who cannot speak for themselves. Either way, you can make a positive impact on the thousands of lives in our community suffering with aphasia by simply knowing more and wearing this wristband. There is no cost. There is no time commitment.
>
> A lack of awareness is as devastating as the disorder itself. My father, like so many others, is too young to live the rest of his life in silent, meaningless captivity. This disorder is not rare, yet people with aphasia often seclude themselves because they don't have the support to navigate their new, unchartered world. Wearing this bracelet can change that. Take the power of knowing more about aphasia, advocate for those who have lost a voice, and be the reason someone finds a new purpose for living.[18]

The speaker effectively closes the loop by suggesting that audience members "wear the wristband in honor of my father" and reminding them that "my father, like so many others, is too young to live the rest of his life in silent, meaningless captivity." Using this technique enables the speaker to urge her audience members to "be the reason someone finds a new purpose for living" in a very personal, eloquent way.

Make sure to close the loop every time you end a speech. By connecting your introduction with your conclusion, you will make your main idea easier to understand and remember.

Discussion Questions

1. What is powerful language?
2. How can you use images to narrow the distance between you and your audience?
3. How do images differ from symbols?
4. How do you create a "moment"?
5. Why is it important to make your characters neither too vague nor too specific?
6. What are the components of a plot?
7. Why do you have to delineate the moral of your anecdote?
8. What is the difference between anaphora and epistrophe?
9. Why is alliteration an effective repetition technique?
10. How do you "close the loop"?

PART 5

DELIVERING SPECIALIZED SPEECHES

Impromptu Speeches

Most of the speaking that you do on a daily basis involves speaking extemporaneously. Whether you are answering a question in class or responding to a colleague during a meeting, your goal is always the same—to convey leadership. You want to show your audience members that you can quickly synthesize a question and present an engaging view.

Keep in mind that you don't need to share *everything* that you know about a specific problem or issue. You simply want to provide a brief, but compelling response that addresses your key idea or position. You can always follow up with more details when addressing a follow-up question.

As you are speaking, remember to stay focused on the main message that you want to convey. Richard Zeoli points out that "it is [easy] for a speaker to become distracted by a tough question or a question that seems to come from left field and throws the speaker for a loop."[1] Although some audience members may pose challenging questions, you must stay on message at all times. Stay calm and in control so you can provide an answer that conveys leadership.

Most importantly, make sure to talk about what *you* think and what *you* feel. According to Shel Leanne, personalizing your message helps establish authority and credibility:

The skilled communicator keeps things personal by leveraging personal pronouns—"I," "you," and "we"—to connect more closely with audience members, establishing a sense of one-to-one conversation. They talk about their own experiences to give power and authority to their words, so listeners understand, "She's been there; she knows."[2]

Don't just speak in generalizations; use personal anecdotes and examples to make your response powerful. Your audience members will admire you for your conviction and will reward you with their trust.

There are four impromptu speaking frameworks that you can use to answer a wide variety of questions: "Providing the Details," "Breaking Up the Question," "Shrinking the Topic," and "Shifting the Focus."[3] Practice using these frameworks whenever you can so you are ready to deliver powerful, off-the-cuff responses when it really counts.

Providing the Details

The first type of impromptu speaking framework is called "Providing the Details." You want to provide the details when you are relaying facts about something that happened. You essentially want to explain *who* was involved, *what* happened, *where* it happened, *when* it happened, *why* it happened, and *how* it happened.

Many speakers only address the *who*, *what*, *where*, and *when* in their responses, but powerful public speakers remember to address the *why* and *how* as well. It is much easier to explain the basics of a situation than to explain why it happened and how it happened. Nevertheless, the *why* and *how* are essential components of a complete answer.

Think back to elementary school. Do you remember when your teacher taught you to answer questions in complete sentences? She would ask, "Where is your homework assignment?" And you would respond, "At home." Then she would tell you to answer in a complete sentence, and you would respond, "I left my homework assignment at home this morning."

Notice that the second response is much clearer than the first because it explains *who* was involved ("I"), *what* happened ("left my homework assignment"), *where* it happened ("at home"), and *when* it happened ("this morning").

If you were asked this same question today, you could strengthen your answer by addressing the *why* and *how* as well. Consider the following response:

> I left my homework assignment at home this morning. I typically organize my assignments into different colored folders, but I was running so late that I accidentally grabbed the wrong folder on my way out the door.

This response is much clearer because it explains *why* it happened ("I was running so late") and *how* it happened ("I accidentally grabbed the wrong folder on my way out the door"). Of course, your teacher might still question whether you actually completed the assignment!

If a colleague asks you what happened during a meeting or a friend asks you what you did over the weekend, provide the details. Paint a clear picture that includes *who, what, where, when, why,* and *how*.

Breaking Up the Question

When you need to share your perspective on a complex or multifaceted issue, you can leverage an impromptu speaking framework called "Breaking Up the Question." This framework helps you separate the question into its component parts and address each part in a structured way.

Imagine that you are running for political office in a large city. What would you say if a reporter walked up to you and asked, "Do you believe that we should build a bridge connecting the airport to the train station?" Sure, you could just say "yes" or "no," but if you want to convey leadership, you would need to support your position with sufficient evidence.

To answer this question powerfully, you must first present your position up front. Don't explain your position until you present your position. You either want to say, "Yes, I feel strongly that we should build the bridge," or "No, it is not a good idea to build the bridge."

Once you have presented your position, you will need to provide a brief, but systematic rationale that helps your audience understand why you feel the way you do. You will ensure that your rationale is crisp if you use a logic model such as *costs vs. benefits, past vs. present, problem vs. solution, us vs. them, or ideal vs. real*. These logic models are essentially guides that you can use to keep your rationale on track. It is important to note that there are many different types of logic models and that some logic models are more effective in certain situations.

Let's look at a sample response using the *costs vs. benefits* logic model:

> Yes, I feel strongly that we should build the bridge. Although building the bridge will be expensive, we will provide better service to and from the airport and support the develop-ment of large tracts of land around the train station.

The speaker clearly expresses her support for the proposal and then discusses the costs and benefits associated with that position. Notice, however, that she crafts her response in such a way that the benefits appear to outweigh the costs.

Let's look at another sample response using the *ideal vs. real* logic model:

> No, it is not a good idea to build the bridge. I really wish that we could fund the bridge project since it would provide better service to and from the airport and support the de-velopment of large tracts of land around the train station. But we're facing tough economic times right now, so we must keep our focus on creating jobs and helping small businesses.

In this example, the speaker clearly expresses his opposition to the proposal and then draws a distinction between what is ideal and what is real. He acknowledges that he would like to support the project, but that the reality of the economic situation makes his position more sensible.

The next time you are asked to share your view on a complex or multifaceted issue, break up the question into its component parts. Decide how you feel, and share your perspective up front. Then use an appropriate logic model to present a compelling rationale.

Shrinking the Topic

If you are presented with a broad question, you can use an impromptu speaking framework called "Shrinking the Topic." You can tackle broad questions by responding to the original question at a high level and then building a bridge to the specific area that you want to address.

I often ask my students a simple, but important question: "What are your goals?" I'm interested in how they plan to use their public speaking skills to change minds and change hearts. After taking my course, my students realize that the best way to answer this question is to shrink the topic.

Here is one possible response:

> There's a lot that I want to accomplish. But my main goal right now is putting together a solid presentation for the case competition finals next week. I really want to impress the panel of judges and win a scholarship.

Notice that the speaker first responds to the original question at a high level: "There's a lot that I want to accomplish." Then he builds a bridge to the specific area that he wants to address—his commitment to "putting together a solid presentation for the case competition finals next week."

Let's consider another example. Suppose you are asked, "What makes the University of Maryland such a great institution?" Given that there are likely many reasons that the University of Maryland is a great institution, you should shrink the topic.

Consider the following response:

> The University of Maryland is a fantastic institution that offers all sorts of opportunities. I get to interact with outstanding professors who are producing cutting-edge research. Even though I'm only an undergraduate student, my professors are really receptive to my interest in research and have invited me to work with them on exciting projects.

As in the previous example, you should first respond to the original question at a high level: "The University of Maryland is a fantastic institution that offers all sorts of opportunities." Then you should build a bridge to the specific area that you want to address—the outstanding faculty, for instance.

Whenever you are asked a broad question, remember to shrink the topic. By using this framework, you will be able to deliver a more focused response that addresses a specific element you feel is important.

Shifting the Focus

Occasionally, someone will ask a question that you don't want to address because it is inappropriate, controversial, or off-topic. You can use an impromptu speaking framework called "Shifting the Focus" to dodge these questions without disrespecting the speaker.

One way to shift the focus is to address a related topic. Let's say a politician is asked whether or not he supports gay marriage.

Consider this possible response:

> I firmly believe in the importance of equality. I am proud of my long record of support for the lesbian, gay, bisexual, and

transgender community, and I pledge to continue to support legislation that ensures all Americans are treated equally and fairly under the law.

In this example, the politician talks about his "long record of support for the lesbian, gay, bisexual, and transgender community," but he doesn't specifically express a position on gay marriage. Instead, he addresses a related topic—the importance of equality.

Another way to shift the focus is to defer the topic. Consider what you would say if you were leading a discussion about study abroad programs, and one of your audience members asked you about the courses that you took to improve your language skills. You might respond, "I'm happy to answer that question after the meeting, but right now, I want to tell you about three exciting study abroad opportunities."

Notice that this response allows you to focus on what *you* want to talk about—travel abroad opportunities—without marginalizing the audience member. There is nothing wrong with deferring a question until you are ready to address it.

It is important to point out that you shouldn't use this framework to avoid answering a relevant or important question. Clearly, there will be times when you should say, "I'm not exactly sure, but I would be happy to research that issue and get back to you with a response." But if someone poses a question that you don't want to or shouldn't answer, remain calm and shift the focus.

Persuasive Speeches

Persuasion is a central part of our daily lives. We rely on our persuasive skills to convince our friends to eat at a specific restaurant, convince our teachers to accept a late assignment, or convince our boss to give us a raise. Indeed, we are constantly trying to persuade other people to accept our point of view.

Persuasion is defined as the process of convincing other people to agree with a particular perspective. As Dan O'Hair, Hannah Rubenstein, and Rob Stewart explain, persuasive speakers leverage two interrelated components—logic and emotion—to build a strong case:

> Persuasive speeches are built upon arguments—stated positions, with support, for or against an idea or issue. Appealing to reason and logic … is important in gaining agreement for your position; it is especially critical when asking listeners to reach a conclusion regarding a complicated issue or to take a specific action. To truly persuade listeners to care about your argument, however, you must also appeal to their emotions … Feelings such as pride, love, anger, shame, and fear underlie many of our actions and motivate us to think and feel as we do.[4]

Given that different people find different types of arguments compelling, you should include both logical and emotional arguments. You certainly can use facts and figures to explain why your position makes sense, but you must also use imagery and anecdotes to illustrate why it really matters. According to novelist Philip Pullman, "'Thou shalt not' might reach the head, but it takes 'Once upon a time' to reach the heart."[5]

Ultimately, the key to crafting a powerful persuasive speech is to develop the mindset of a salesperson. Your objective is to convince as many of your audience members as possible to "buy" the product or idea that you are selling. You can motivate your audience members to sign on the dotted line by identifying a narrow problem, exploring a potential solution, and introducing a specific action.

Identifying a Narrow Problem

The first step in the persuasion process is to determine what issue you want to address. What is it about the world that you want to change? You can speak about any issue that interests you, as long as you frame it as an important problem.

Let's say that you are concerned about protecting the environment. Although you may feel strongly that this issue is important, your audience members won't necessarily feel the same way. This is why you must frame the issue as a problem and show them that there is something wrong, unjust, or unfair happening in the world that they can help make "right."

The best way to frame the issue as a problem is to think about why the issue matters in the first place. As an environmentally conscious citizen, you might say to yourself: "We are using and disposing of materials without considering the environmental impact of our actions. We simply are producing an unimaginable amount of waste." This statement reveals a specific problem—the excessive amount of waste production.

Once you have identified a problem, you must determine which aspect of the problem you want to address. Don't try to fix the whole world in a single speech. Pick one component, and focus on it.

Douglas Fraleigh and Joseph Tuman posit that narrowing down the problem will help you keep your audience members' attention:

It allows you to fit your speech into the available time. Whether you are speaking in a classroom or in your community, it is inconsiderate to take more than the time allocated for your presentation, and audiences may stop listening if you exceed the time limit. And resist any urge to speak fast, or to cover each idea sketchily, in order to say everything you had planned. Audiences don't respond well to those tactics, either.[6]

You must identify one aspect of the problem that you can easily explain to your audience. In this case, you might say to yourself: "One reason that we produce so much waste is that we don't recycle enough of the materials that we consume." This realization has helped you narrow down the problem to a much simpler idea—the lack of recycling.

You can make this problem even more specific by customizing your message. You could deliver a persuasive speech on "the lack of recycling" to any audience. You want to make the problem relevant to *your* audience.

One way to customize the message is to speak about the lack of recycling in the community where your audience members work and live. Consider the following example:

> Americans produce about four pounds of garbage per person every day. In Lakewood, Ohio, our 150,000 residents produce 46 million pounds of trash annually, filling our city's only landfill with more than 20,000 tons of trash per year. Last year, the city launched a recycling program to reduce the amount of waste that ends up in our landfill. Unfortunately, only 46 percent of Lakewood residents elected to participate in the program.[7]

This introduction effectively narrows down a national problem (the excessive amount of garbage produced every day) to a pressing issue facing the city of Lakewood (the lack of participation in the city's recycling program). Moreover, it customizes the message by referring to "our 150,000 residents," "our city's only landfill," and "Lakewood residents."

Whenever you deliver a persuasive speech, remember to frame your issue as a problem. Then narrow down the problem as much as possible, and customize your message to your audience.

Exploring a Potential Solution

The second step in the persuasion process is to tell your audience members how to address the problem that you identified. Your audience members may not have been thinking about the problem until you started talking about it, but they now realize that the problem exists and that it is important.

Jeanette and Roy Henderson compare the persuasion process to the sales process:

> All of the best advertising campaigns unabashedly capitalize on first defining this undefined need, then providing the information necessary to obtain it, whatever *it* may be. In fact, whenever a producer or salesman convinces a consumer to buy his product, he is fundamentally establishing the same kind of Alliance that you want to initiate with your [audience]: Buy our product, and your newly discovered need (the one we've just now told you about) will be satisfied.[8]

Although your audience members may want to hear about your solution, they will only "buy" it if they understand what it is and how it works. Don't overwhelm your listeners with a "phased process" or a "multi-year strategy." Instead, select one easy-to-understand solution, and help them visualize the impact that it will have on their lives.

Imagine that you are speaking to a group of mothers with young children about the importance of child passenger safety. You have cited statistics showing that four children are killed, and 504 children are injured every day in motor vehicle accidents.[9] As a result, your audience members have begun thinking about their own children and how they can keep them safe. You should address their concerns by exploring a potential solution:

> The proper use of child car seats is one of the simplest and most effective methods available for protecting the lives of our young children in the event of a motor vehicle crash. There are many different types of child car seats on the market today. Each one must meet federal standards, and all provide good protection for your child when used correctly. The "right" seat for you is largely a matter of personal choice. Choose a seat that fits your child and your car, read the instructions carefully, and use the seat correctly on every trip. When used correctly, a car seat will hold your child in place and protect your child from bodily harm in the event of a crash.[10]

Notice that this example highlights a single, simple solution—using a car seat—and clearly explains how the solution addresses the problem: "The proper use of child car seats is one of the simplest and most effective methods available for protecting the lives of our young children in the event of a motor vehicle crash." This example also enables your audience members to visualize the impact of using a car seat: "a car seat will hold your child in place and protect your child from bodily harm in the event of a crash."

Remember that your audience members will only find your solution credible if it directly addresses the problem that you identified. Don't settle on the first solution that pops into your head; discuss the solution that has the best chance of working. Then help your audience members visualize what the world will look like once the solution is implemented.

Introducing a Specific Action

The final step in the persuasion process is to convince your audience members to take action. You already have explored the merits of a potential solution. Now you must introduce a very specific action and explain why it is worthwhile.

Let's say that you are speaking to a group of classmates about the benefits of organic fruits and vegetables. You have explained that conventionally grown fruits and vegetables contain toxic pesticide residues that may cause significant health problems.[11] To address this problem, you have proposed that consumers avoid purchasing non-organic fruits and vegetables with high pesticide residues. Now you must tell your classmates what action they should take:

> After my speech, I will hand out a shopping guide that lists the 12 fruits and vegetables that have the highest pesticide residues. Take this guide with you every time you head to the supermarket, and refer to it when you are in the produce section. You can lower your pesticide consumption by nearly four-fifths by avoiding non-organic versions of the fruits and vegetables that are on the list.[12]

This example highlights a very specific action: "Take this guide with you every time you head to the supermarket, and refer to it when you are in the produce section." It also explicitly underscores the value of the proposed action by noting that audience members can reduce their "pesticide consumption by nearly four-fifths by avoiding non-organic versions of the fruits and vegetables that are on the list."

Be sure to introduce a specific action at the end of every persuasive speech. You could ask your audience members to contact their elected officials, make a donation, or attend an upcoming event. As Lyman MacInnis reminds us, "In a talk to motivate, if you don't ask you probably won't get. You have to let your audience know exactly and clearly what it is that you want them to do or not do."[13] Ask your audience members to take a specific action, and then explain how the action will make an important impact.

Inspirational Speeches

As a leader, you will often have to motivate your audience members to achieve something great—something that seems out of reach. Your job is to eliminate the words "can't," "don't," and "won't" from their vocabulary and push them to go further than they ever thought was possible.

Inspiration is defined as the process of lifting peoples' sights and spirits and enabling them to achieve challenging or irrational goals. As Dan O'Hair, Hannah Rubenstein, and Rob Stewart explain, inspirational speeches "touch on deep feelings in the audience. Through emotional force, they urge us toward purer motives and harder effort and remind us of a common good."[14]

Some people use the terms "persuasion" and "inspiration" interchangeably, and others confuse "inspiration" with "charisma." The truth is that inspiration is very different from persuasion, and delivering an inspirational speech involves much more than exuding charisma. Inspiration involves crafting and delivering arguments of the heart.

In *The Leadership Challenge*, James Kouzes and Barry Posner explain that inspirational speakers talk about ideals and dreams to mobilize their audience members to act:

> Visions are about ideals—hopes, dreams, and aspirations. They're about our strong desire to achieve something great. They're ambitious. They're expressions of optimism. Can you

imagine a leader enlisting others in a cause by saying, "I'd like you to join me in doing the ordinary better"? Not likely. Visions necessarily stretch us to imagine exciting possibilities, breakthrough technologies, or revolutionary social change.[15]

Inspirational speakers don't just talk about their vision; they make their audience believe that their vision is achievable. They take their audience on an inspirational journey by holding out hope, making the impossible appear possible, and believing in their message.

Holding Out Hope

A powerful way to inspire your audience members is to hold out hope. You can create a sense of possibility by candidly discussing the current situation and providing specific reasons that your audience members should push forward.

Imagine that you are the CEO of a large company that has struggled to deliver solid financial results for the past few quarters. You could inspire your employees to redouble their efforts next quarter by holding out hope:

> I know we've had a pretty rough ride this year. Our revenues are down, and our stock price is down. Although we are operating in a challenging business environment, I'm confident that we have the best people, the best product, and the best strategy. If we really work hard and focus on our strengths, we will not only have an outstanding fourth quarter, but we will also become one of the strongest players in the industry.

As this example illustrates, you should start by candidly acknowledging the current situation: "I know we've had a pretty rough ride this year. Our revenues are down, and our stock price is down." However, you shouldn't dwell on these issues. You should quickly turn your attention to the specific reasons that your employees should remain hopeful: "we have the best people, the best product, and the best strategy."

Don't ask your audience members to trust you because you have a lot of experience with challenging situations or because you have put together an effective plan. Make sure to offer *specific* reasons that your audience members should keep working or keep fighting.

According to Carmine Gallo, inspirational speakers know that they must convey optimism, even if the chances of success are slim:

> You are the leader people want to believe in. Your customers and employees are bombarded by bad news—the credit crunch, a housing slump, an economic slowdown—but they are eager to hear something positive. That doesn't mean leaders stick their heads in the sand—far from it. Inspiring leaders acknowledge the situation but also remind people of reasons to be optimistic.[16]

As Gallo points out, inspirational speakers stay positive no matter what challenge they are facing. Inspirational speakers hold out hope.

Making the Impossible Appear Possible

Another way to inspire your audience members is to make the impossible appear possible—to make something really hard seem much more achievable.

It is quite difficult to imagine a world free of discrimination, a society where every child has access to a quality education, or a company that achieves 50 percent revenue growth year after year. Nevertheless, inspirational speakers motivate their audience members to work toward these goals by emphasizing possibility. As Kouzes and Posner note, "leaders are *possibility* thinkers, not *probability* thinkers.[17]

The first technique that you can use to make the impossible appear possible is to discuss historical success anecdotes—moments of achievement in a nation's or an organization's history that the audience members know about or remember. Talking about these powerful moments will prompt your audience members to think, "If we did it before, we can do it again." Let's look at an example.

When Senator Barack Obama lost the 2008 presidential primary in New Hampshire, he didn't concede defeat and end his campaign. He realized that his journey was improbable, that it seemed almost impossible for an African American to become president of the United States. But he made his audience members feel like change was possible by referencing significant historical achievements:

> For when we have faced down impossible odds, when we've been told we're not ready or that we shouldn't try or that we can't, generations of Americans have responded with a simple creed that sums up the spirit of a people: Yes, we can. Yes, we can. Yes, we can.
>
> It was a creed written into the founding documents that declared the destiny of a nation: Yes, we can. It was whispered by slaves and abolitionists as they blazed a trail towards freedom through the darkest of nights: Yes, we can. It was sung by immigrants as they struck out from distant shores and pioneers who pushed westward against an unforgiving wilderness: Yes, we can.
>
> It was the call of workers who organized, women who reached for the ballot, a president who chose the moon as our new frontier, and a king who took us to the mountaintop and pointed the way to the promised land: Yes, we can, to justice and equality. Yes, we can, to opportunity and prosperity. Yes, we can heal this nation. Yes, we can repair this world. Yes, we can.[18]

Senator Obama evokes feelings of possibility and hope by citing a variety of moments when Americans "faced down impossible odds." He talks about "slaves and abolitionists" who "blazed a trail towards freedom through the darkest of nights," "pioneers who pushed westward against an unforgiving wilderness," and a "king who took us to the mountaintop and pointed the way to the promised land." By invoking powerful historical moments, Senator Obama creates forward momentum and makes his audience members feel like they too can accomplish something monumental.

A second technique that you can use to make the impossible appear possible is to break your goal into logical steps. Essentially, you want to delineate the specific steps that your audience members can take to inch closer to the finish line.

Let's say that you want to inspire a group of co-workers who have never run more than a couple of miles to complete a 26.2-mile marathon. You can make the goal seem more realistic by breaking it into logical steps:

> I know that running a marathon seems impossible right now, but we can make progress toward our goal by meeting tomorrow at 7 A.M. to walk one mile. After we finish the walk, we will meet with a nutritionist and a personal trainer to learn healthy eating and exercise habits. Then we can figure out when to plan our first short run.

Although your co-workers may still doubt their ability to complete the marathon, they will feel empowered to begin the journey. After all, they will be able to envision themselves "meeting tomorrow at 7 A.M. to walk one mile" and meeting "with a nutritionist and a personal trainer to learn healthy eating and exercise habits."

Inspirational speakers don't believe in impossibility. They make their audience members feel like success is possible by discussing historical success anecdotes and breaking the goal into logical steps.

Believing in Your Message

The most powerful way to inspire your audience members is to show them that you are deeply committed to a particular goal. You can't just talk about possibility and hope from a distance; you must open up and share what is in your heart. You must "get lost in your message" by feeling, not just saying, your words and by sharing your true emotions with your audience.

As Kouzes and Posner point out, it is very easy for audience members to determine whether or not a speaker believes in his message:

> We're all able to spot lack of sincerity in others. We detect it in their voices; we observe it in their eyes; we notice it in their posture. We each have a sixth sense for deceit and can usually tell the fraudulent from the real. So there's a very fundamental question that a leader must ask before attempting to enlist others: "What do I believe in?" The true force that attracts others is the force of the heart. Inspirational presentations are heart to heart, spirit to spirit, life to life. It's when you share what's in your soul that you can truly move others.[19]

When you believe in your message, you naturally ooze passion. Your audience members will feel this passion and, in turn, feel closer and more connected to you.

J.K. Rowling, author of the popular *Harry Potter* series, demonstrated a strong belief in her message when she spoke at the Harvard University Commencement Exercises in 2008:

> So I think it fair to say that by any conventional measure, a mere seven years after my graduation day, I had failed on an epic scale. An exceptionally short-lived marriage had imploded, and I was jobless, a lone parent, and as poor as it is possible to be in modern Britain, without being homeless. The fears that my parents had had for me, and that I had had for myself, had both come to pass, and by every usual standard, I was the biggest failure I knew.
>
> Now, I am not going to stand here and tell you that failure is fun. That period of my life was a dark one, and I had no idea that there was going to be what the press has since represented as a kind of fairy tale resolution. I had no idea then

how far the tunnel extended, and for a long time, any light at the end of it was a hope rather than a reality.

So why do I talk about the benefits of failure? Simply because failure meant a stripping away of the inessential. I stopped pretending to myself that I was anything other than what I was, and began to direct all my energy into finishing the only work that mattered to me. Had I really succeeded at anything else, I might never have found the determination to succeed in the one arena I believed I truly belonged. I was set free, because my greatest fear had been realised, and I was still alive, and I still had a daughter whom I adored, and I had an old typewriter and a big idea. And so rock bottom became the solid foundation on which I rebuilt my life.[20]

Notice that Rowling doesn't talk about failure from a distance or hide behind other peoples' failures. She candidly admits that her own "marriage had imploded," that she was "jobless, a lone parent, and as poor as it is possible to be in modern Britain, without being homeless," and that she "was the biggest failure" she knew. She also "gets lost in her message" by opening up about how difficult it was for her to stop pretending that she hadn't "failed on an epic scale."

Indeed, inspirational speakers convey credibility and authenticity by sharing their true emotions with their audience. But they don't simply talk about how they feel. They show their audience that they are personally committed to a particular goal by taking the first step.

Imagine that you want to inspire some of your peers to study for an exam the following afternoon. Although your peers want to do well, they are pretty tired after a long day of classes and feel like they already know enough of the material to earn a decent grade. Show them that you believe in the cause by taking the first step:

Look, I know you're all tired. I'm tired too. But I'm going to be at the library tonight at 9 P.M., and I'm going to stay there until I understand how this stuff works. I really want to ace this exam, and I hope that you'll join me tonight so we can all earn an "A."

It is much more effective to say, "I'm going to be at the library tonight," than it is to talk about the importance of studying. By taking the first step, you could show your peers that you are serious about acing the exam.

Many speakers talk about what others should do to support a cause, but rarely do these speakers engage in those activities themselves. Inspirational speakers know that "doing" matters more than "talking," so they set an example that others can follow. They show up even if they're busy and push forward even if they're tired. They don't tell people where to go or what to do. They take the first step themselves and inspire others to follow them.

If you're talking about raising money, pull whatever money you have out of your wallet and make a public donation. If you're talking about lobbying for a change, explain where you will be and when you will be there, and invite your audience members to stand alongside you. Take a simple, concrete action that shows them you are serious about making an impact.

Inspirational speakers motivate their audience to act by demonstrating that they are deeply committed to a particular goal. They don't talk about hope and possibility from a distance. They "get lost in their message" and take the first step.

Discussion Questions

1. What is your main objective when you are delivering an impromptu speech?
2. How does "breaking up the question" differ from "shrinking the topic"?
3. When should you "shift the focus"?
4. How can you craft compelling persuasive arguments?
5. Why should you frame an issue as an important problem?
6. How can you convince your audience members to "buy" your potential solution?
7. What is the difference between persuasion and inspiration?
8. Why is it important to hold out hope?
9. How do you make the impossible appear possible?
10. What does it mean to "believe in your message"?

Appendix:
Powerful Public Speeches

I have selected a variety of powerful public speeches that incorporate many of the techniques in this book. As you read through these examples, see if you can identify the techniques that the speakers use to captivate their audience members and demonstrate their capacity to lead. Then apply these same techniques to your own speeches, so you can change minds and change hearts every time you speak.

Impromptu Speeches

Persuasive Speeches

Inspirational Speeches

Statement on the
Assassination of Martin Luther King Jr.

Senator Robert F. Kennedy
Indianapolis, Indiana
April 4, 1968

I have bad news for you, for all of our fellow citizens, and people who love peace all over the world, and that is that Martin Luther King was shot and killed tonight.

Martin Luther King dedicated his life to love and to justice for his fellow human beings, and he died because of that effort.

In this difficult day, in this difficult time for the United States, it is perhaps well to ask what kind of a nation we are and what direction we want to move in. For those of you who are black—considering the evidence there evidently is that there were white people who were responsible—you can be filled with bitterness, with hatred, and a desire for revenge. We can move in that direction as a country, in great polarization—black people amongst black, white people amongst white, filled with hatred toward one another.

Or we can make an effort, as Martin Luther King did, to understand and to comprehend, and to replace that violence, that stain of bloodshed that has spread across our land, with an effort to understand with compassion and love.

For those of you who are black and are tempted to be filled with hatred and distrust at the injustice of such an act, against all white people, I can only say that I feel in my own heart the same kind of feeling. I had a member of my family killed, but he was killed by a white man. But we have to make an effort in the United States, we have to make an effort to understand, to go beyond these rather difficult times.

My favorite poet was Aeschylus. He wrote: "In our sleep, pain which cannot forget falls drop by drop upon the heart until, in our own despair, against our will, comes wisdom through the awful grace of God."

What we need in the United States is not division; what we need in the United States is not hatred; what we need in the United States is not violence or lawlessness; but love and wisdom, and compassion toward one another, and a feeling of justice toward those who still suffer within our country, whether they be white or they be black.

So I shall ask you tonight to return home, to say a prayer for the family of Martin Luther King, that's true, but more importantly to say a prayer for our own country, which all of us love—a prayer for understanding and that compassion of which I spoke.

We can do well in this country. We will have difficult times; we've had difficult times in the past; we will have difficult times in the future. It is not the end of violence; it is not the end of lawlessness; it is not the end of disorder.

But the vast majority of white people and the vast majority of black people in this country want to live together, want to improve the quality of our life, and want justice for all human beings who abide in our land.

Let us dedicate ourselves to what the Greeks wrote so many years ago: to tame the savageness of man and make gentle the life of this world.

Let us dedicate ourselves to that, and say a prayer for our country and for our people.

Bullhorn Salute to
Ground Zero Rescue Workers

President George W. Bush
New York, New York
September 14, 2001

CROWD: U.S.A.! U.S.A.!

THE PRESIDENT: Thank you all. I, uh, I want you all to know—

Comment: Louder.

THE PRESIDENT: I can't go any louder. (Laughter.) I want you all to know that America today—America today is on bended knee in prayer for the people whose lives were lost here, for the workers who work here, for the families who mourn. This nation stands with the good people of New York City, and New Jersey and Connecticut, as we mourn the loss of thousands of our citizens.

Comment: I can't hear you.

THE PRESIDENT: I can hear you. (Applause.) I can hear you. The rest of the world hears you. (Applause.) And the people—and the people who knocked these buildings down will hear all of us soon. (Applause.)

CROWD: U.S.A.! U.S.A.!

THE PRESIDENT: The nation—the nation sends its love and compassion to everybody who is here. Thank you for your hard work. Thank you for making the nation proud. And may God bless America. (Applause.)

CROWD: U.S.A.! U.S.A.!

Remarks at the 90th
Convocation of Vanderbilt University

President John F. Kennedy
Nashville, Tennessee
May 18, 1963

Mr. Chancellor, Mr. Vanderbilt, Senator Kefauver, Senator Gore, Congressman Fulton, Congressman Evins, Congressman Bass, Congressman Everett, Tom Murray, distinguished guests, members of the judiciary, the Army Corps of Engineers of the Tennessee Valley:

I first of all want to express my warm appreciation to the Governor and to the Mayor of this State and city and to the people for a very generous welcome, and particularly to all those young men and women who lined the street and played music for us as we drove into this stadium. We are glad they are here with us, and we feel the musical future of this city and State is assured.

Many things bring us together today. We are saluting the 90th anniversary of Vanderbilt University, which has grown from a small Tennessee university and institution to one of our Nation's greatest, with 7 different colleges, and with more than half of its 4200 students from outside of the State of Tennessee.

And we are saluting the 30th anniversary of the Tennessee Valley Authority, which transformed a parched, depressed, and floodravaged region into a fertile, productive center of industry, science, and agriculture.

We are saluting—by initiating construction of a dam in his name—a great Tennessee statesman, Cordell Hull, the father of reciprocal trade, the grandfather of the United Nations, the Secretary of State who presided over the transformation of this Nation from a life of isolation and almost indifference to a state of responsible world leadership.

And finally, we are saluting—by the recognition of a forthcoming dam in his name—J. Percy Priest, a former colleague of mine in the House of Representatives, who represented this district, this State, and this Nation in the Congress for 16 turbulent years—years which witnessed the crumbling of empires, the splitting of the atom, the conquest of one threat to freedom, and the emergence of still another.

If there is one unchanging theme that runs throughout these separate stories, it is that everything changes but change itself. We live in an age of movement and change, both evolutionary and revolutionary, both good and evil—and in such an age a university has a special obligation to hold fast to the best of the past and move fast to the best of the future.

Nearly 100 years ago Prince Bismarck said that one-third of the students of German universities broke down from overwork, another third broke down from dissipation, and the other third ruled Germany. I do not know which third of the student body of Vanderbilt is here today, but I am confident we are talking to the future rulers of Tennessee and America in the spirit of this university.

The essence of Vanderbilt is still learning, the essence of its outlook is still liberty, and liberty and learning will be and must be the touchstones of Vanderbilt University and of any free university in this country or the world. I say two touchstones, yet they are almost inseparable, inseparable if not indistinguishable, for liberty without learning is always in peril, and learning without liberty is always in vain.

This State, this city, this campus, have stood long for both human rights and human enlightenment—and let that forever be true. This Nation is now engaged in a continuing debate about the rights of a portion of its citizens. That will go on, and those rights will expand until the standard first forged by the Nation's founders has been reached, and all Americans enjoy equal opportunity and liberty under law.

But this Nation was not founded solely on the principle of citizens' rights. Equally important, though too often not discussed, is the citizen's responsibility. For our privileges can be no greater than our obligations. The protection of our rights can endure no longer than the performance of our responsibilities. Each can be neglected only at the peril of the other. I speak to you today, therefore, not of your rights as Americans, but of your responsibilities. They are many in number and different in nature. They do not rest with equal weight upon the shoulders of all. Equality of opportunity does not mean equality of responsibility. All Americans must be responsible citizens, but some must be more responsible than others, by virtue of their public or their private position, their role in the family or community, their prospects for the future, or their legacy from the past.

Increased responsibility goes with increased ability, for "of those to whom much is given, much is required."

Commodore Vanderbilt recognized this responsibility and his recognition made possible the establishment of a great institution of learning for which he will be long remembered after his steamboats and railroads have been forgotten. I speak in particular, therefore, of the responsibility of the educated citizen, including the students, the faculty, and the alumni of this great institution. The creation and maintenance of Vanderbilt University, like that of all great universities, has required considerable effort and expenditure, and I cannot believe that all of this was undertaken merely to give this school's graduates an economic advantage in the life struggle. "Every man sent out from a university," said Professor Woodrow Wilson, "Every man sent out from a university should be a man of his Nation, as well as a man of his time."

You have responsibilities, in short, to use your talents for the benefit of the society which helped develop those talents. You must decide, as Goethe put it, whether you will be an anvil or a hammer, whether you will give to the world in which you were reared and educated the broadest possible benefits of that education. Of the many special obligations incumbent upon an educated citizen, I would cite three as outstanding: your obligation to the pursuit of learning, your obligation to serve the public, your obligation to uphold the law.

If the pursuit of learning is not defended by the educated citizen, it will not be defended at all. For there will always be those who scoff at intellectuals, who cry out against research, who seek to limit our educational system. Modern cynics and skeptics see no more reason for landing a man on the moon, which we shall do, than the cynics and skeptics of half a millennium ago saw for the discovery of this country. They see no harm in paying those to whom they entrust the minds of their children a smaller wage than is paid to those to whom they entrust the care of their plumbing.

But the educated citizen knows how much more there is to know. He knows that "knowledge is power," more so today than ever before. He knows that only an educated and informed people will be a free people, that the ignorance of one voter in a democracy impairs the security of all, and that if we can, as Jefferson put it, "enlighten the people generally … tyranny and the oppressions of mind and body will vanish, like evil spirits at the dawn of day." And, therefore, the educated citizen has a special obligation to encourage the pursuit of learning, to promote exploration of the unknown, to preserve the freedom of inquiry, to support the advancement of research, and to assist at every level of government the improvement of education for all Americans, from grade school to graduate school.

Secondly, the educated citizen has an obligation to serve the public. He may be a precinct worker or President. He may give his talents at the courthouse, the State house, the White House. He may be a civil servant or a Senator, a candidate or a campaign worker, a winner or a loser. But he must be a participant and not a spectator.

"At the Olympic games," Aristotle wrote, "it is not the finest and strongest men who are crowned, but they who enter the lists—for out of these the prize-men are elected. So, too, in life, of the honorable and the good, it is they who act who rightly win the prizes."

I urge all of you today, especially those who are students, to act, to enter the lists of public service and rightly win or lose the prize. For we can have only one form of aristocracy in this country, as Jefferson wrote long ago in rejecting John Adams' suggestion of an artificial aristocracy of wealth and birth. It is, he wrote, the natural aristocracy of character and talent, and the best form of government, he added, was that which selected these men for positions of responsibility.

I would hope that all educated citizens would fulfill this obligation—in politics, in Government, here in Nashville, here in this State, in the Peace Corps, in the Foreign Service, in the Government Service, in the Tennessee Valley, in the world. You will find the pressures greater than the pay. You may endure more public attacks than support. But you will have the unequaled satisfaction of knowing that your character and talent are contributing to the direction and success of this free society.

Third, and finally, the educated citizen has an obligation to uphold the law. This is the obligation of every citizen in a free and peaceful society—but the educated citizen has a special responsibility by the virtue of his greater understanding. For whether he has ever studied history or current events, ethics or civics, the rules of a profession or the tools of a trade, he knows that only a respect for the law makes it possible for free men to dwell together in peace and progress.

He knows that law is the adhesive force in the cement of society, creating order out of chaos and coherence in place of anarchy. He knows that for one man to defy a law or court order he does not like is to invite others to defy those which they do not like, leading to a breakdown of all justice and all order. He knows, too, that every fellowman is entitled to be regarded with decency and treated with dignity. Any educated citizen who seeks to subvert the law, to suppress freedom, or to subject other human beings to acts that are less than human, degrades his heritage, ignores his learning, and betrays his obligation.

Certain other societies may respect the rule of force—we respect the rule of law.

The Nation, indeed the whole world, has watched recent events in the United States with alarm and dismay. No one can deny the complexity of the problems involved in assuring to all of our citizens their full rights as Americans. But no one can gainsay the fact that the determination to secure these rights is in the highest traditions of American freedom.

In these moments of tragic disorder, a special burden rests on the educated men and women of our country to reject the temptations of prejudice and violence, and to reaffirm the values of freedom and law on which our free society depends.

When Bishop McTyeire, 90 years ago, proposed it to Commodore Vanderbilt, he said, "Commodore, our country has been torn to pieces by a civil war ... We want to repair this damage." And Commodore Vanderbilt reportedly replied, "I want to unite this country, and all sections of it, so that all our people will be one." His response, his recognition of his obligation and opportunity gave Vanderbilt University not only an endowment but also a mission. Now, 90 years later, in a time of tension, it is more important than ever to unite this country and strengthen these ties so that all of our people will be one.

Ninety years from now I have no doubt that Vanderbilt University will still be fulfilling this mission. It will still uphold learning, encourage public service, and teach respect for the law. It will neither turn its back on proven wisdom or turn its face from newborn challenge. It will still pass on to the youth of our land the full meaning of their rights and their responsibilities. And it will still be teaching the truth—the truth that makes us free and will keep us free.

Thank you.

Oklahoma City Memorial Service Address

President William J. Clinton
Oklahoma City, Oklahoma
April 23, 1995

Thank you very much. Governor Keating and Mrs. Keating, Reverend Graham, to the families of those who have been lost and wounded, to the people of Oklahoma City, who have endured so much, and the people of this wonderful state, to all of you who are here as our fellow Americans.

I am honored to be here today to represent the American people. But I have to tell you that Hillary and I also come as parents, as husband and wife, as people who were your neighbors for some of the best years of our lives.

Today our nation joins with you in grief. We mourn with you. We share your hope against hope that some may still survive. We thank all those who have worked so heroically to save lives and to solve this crime—those here in Oklahoma and those who are all across this great land, and many who left their own lives to come here to work hand in hand with you.

We pledge to do all we can to help you heal the injured, to rebuild this city, and to bring to justice those who did this evil.

This terrible sin took the lives of our American family, innocent children in that building, only because their parents were trying to be good parents as well as good workers; citizens in the building going about their daily business; and many there who served the rest of us—who worked to help the elderly and the disabled, who worked to support our farmers and our veterans, who worked to enforce our laws and to protect us. Let us say clearly, they served us well, and we are grateful.

But for so many of you they were also neighbors and friends. You saw them at church or the PTA meetings, at the civic clubs, at the ball park. You know them in ways that all the rest of America could not.

And to all the members of the families here present who have suffered loss, though we share your grief, your pain is unimaginable, and we know that. We cannot undo it. That is God's work.

Our words seem small beside the loss you have endured. But I found a few I wanted to share today. I've received a lot of letters in these last terrible days. One stood out because it came from a young widow and a mother of three whose own husband was murdered with over 200 other Americans when Pan Am 103 was shot down. Here is what that woman said I should say to you today:

The anger you feel is valid, but you must not allow yourselves to be consumed by it. The hurt you feel must not be allowed to turn into hate, but instead into the search for justice. The loss you feel must not paralyze your own lives. Instead, you must try to pay tribute to your loved ones by continuing to do all the things they left undone, thus ensuring they did not die in vain.

Wise words from one who also knows.

You have lost too much, but you have not lost everything. And you have certainly not lost America, for we will stand with you for as many tomorrows as it takes.

If ever we needed evidence of that, I could only recall the words of Governor and Mrs. Keating. If anybody thinks that Americans are mostly mean and selfish, they ought to come to Oklahoma. (Applause.) If anybody thinks Americans have lost the capacity for love and caring and courage, they ought to come to Oklahoma.

To all my fellow Americans beyond this hall, I say, one thing we owe those who have sacrificed is the duty to purge ourselves of the dark forces which gave rise to this evil. They are forces that threaten our common peace, our freedom, our way of life.

Let us teach our children that the God of comfort is also the God of righteousness. Those who trouble their own house will inherit the wind. Justice will prevail.

Let us let our own children know that we will stand against the forces of fear. When there is talk of hatred, let us stand up and talk against it. When there is talk of violence, let us stand up and talk against it. In the face of death, let us honor life. As St. Paul admonished us, let us not be overcome by evil, but overcome evil with good. Yesterday Hillary and I had the privilege of speaking with some children of other federal employees—children like those who were lost here. And one little girl said something we will never forget. She said, we should all plant a tree in memory of the children. So this morning before we got on the plane to come here, at the White House, we planted a tree in honor of the children of Oklahoma.

It was a dogwood with its wonderful spring flower and its deep, enduring roots. It embodies the lesson of the Psalms—that the life of a good person is like a tree whose leaf does not wither.

My fellow Americans, a tree takes a long time to grow, and wounds take a long time to heal. But we must begin. Those who are lost now belong to God. Some day we will be with them. But until that happens, their legacy must be our lives.

Thank you all, and God bless you.

Remarks at the Tucson Shooting Memorial Service

President Barack Obama
Tucson, Arizona
January 12, 2011

THE PRESIDENT: Thank you. (Applause.) Thank you very much. Please, please be seated. (Applause.)

To the families of those we've lost; to all who called them friends; to the students of this university, the public servants who are gathered here, the people of Tucson and the people of Arizona: I have come here tonight as an American who, like all Americans, kneels to pray with you today and will stand by you tomorrow. (Applause.)

There is nothing I can say that will fill the sudden hole torn in your hearts. But know this: The hopes of a nation are here tonight. We mourn with you for the fallen. We join you in your grief. And we add our faith to yours that Representative Gabrielle Giffords and the other living victims of this tragedy will pull through. (Applause.)

Scripture tells us:

> There is a river whose streams make glad the city of God,
> the holy place where the Most High dwells.
> God is within her, she will not fall;
> God will help her at break of day.

On Saturday morning, Gabby, her staff and many of her constituents gathered outside a supermarket to exercise their right to peaceful assembly and free speech. (Applause.) They were fulfilling a central tenet of the democracy envisioned by our founders—representatives of the people answering questions to their constituents, so as to carry their concerns back to our nation's capital. Gabby called it "Congress on Your Corner"—just an updated version of government of and by and for the people. (Applause.)

And that quintessentially American scene, that was the scene that was shattered by a gunman's bullets. And the six people who lost their lives on Saturday—they, too, represented what is best in us, what is best in America. (Applause.)

Judge John Roll served our legal system for nearly 40 years. (Applause.) A graduate of this university and a graduate of this law school—(applause)—Judge Roll was recommended for the federal bench by John McCain 20 years ago—(applause)—appointed by President George H.W. Bush and rose to become Arizona's chief federal judge. (Applause.)

His colleagues described him as the hardest-working judge within the Ninth Circuit. He was on his way back from attending Mass, as he did every day, when he decided to stop by and say hi to his representative. John is survived by his loving wife, Maureen, his three sons and his five beautiful grandchildren. (Applause.)

George and Dorothy Morris—"Dot" to her friends—were high school sweethearts who got married and had two daughters. They did everything together—traveling the open road in their RV, enjoying what their friends called a 50-year honeymoon. Saturday morning, they went by the Safeway to hear what their congresswoman had to say. When gunfire rang out, George, a former Marine, instinctively tried to shield his wife. (Applause.) Both were shot. Dot passed away.

A New Jersey native, Phyllis Schneck retired to Tucson to beat the snow. But in the summer, she would return East, where her world revolved around her three children, her seven grandchildren and 2-year-old great-granddaughter. A gifted quilter, she'd often work under a favorite tree, or sometimes she'd sew aprons with the logos of the Jets and the Giants—(laughter)—to give out at the church where she volunteered. A Republican, she took a liking to Gabby, and wanted to get to know her better. (Applause.)

Dorwan and Mavy Stoddard grew up in Tucson together—about 70 years ago. They moved apart and started their own respective families. But after both were widowed they found their way back here, to, as one of Mavy's daughters put it, "be boyfriend and girlfriend again." (Laughter.)

When they weren't out on the road in their motor home, you could find them just up the road, helping folks in need at the Mountain Avenue Church of Christ. A retired construction worker, Dorwan spent his spare time fixing up the church along with his dog, Tux. His final act of selflessness was to dive on top of his wife, sacrificing his life for hers. (Applause.)

Everything—everything—Gabe Zimmerman did, he did with passion. (Applause.) But his true passion was helping people. As Gabby's outreach director, he made the cares of thousands of her constituents his own, seeing to it that seniors got the Medicare benefits that they had earned, that veterans got the medals and the care that they deserved, that government was working for ordinary folks. He died doing what he loved—talking with people and seeing how he could help. And Gabe is survived by his parents, Ross and Emily, his brother, Ben, and his fiancée, Kelly, who he planned to marry next year. (Applause.)

And then there is nine-year-old Christina Taylor Green. Christina was an A student; she was a dancer; she was a gymnast; she was a swimmer. She decided that she wanted to be the first woman to play in the Major Leagues, and as the only girl on her Little League team, no one put it past her. (Applause.)

She showed an appreciation for life uncommon for a girl her age. She'd remind her mother, "We are so blessed. We have the best life." And she'd pay those blessings back by participating in a charity that helped children who were less fortunate.

Our hearts are broken by their sudden passing. Our hearts are broken—and yet, our hearts also have reason for fullness. Our hearts are full of hope and thanks for the 13 Americans who survived the shooting, including the congresswoman many of them went to see on Saturday.

I have just come from the University Medical Center, just a mile from here, where our friend Gabby courageously fights to recover even as we speak. And I want to tell you—her husband Mark is here and he allows me to share this with you—right after we went to visit, a few minutes after we left her room and some of her colleagues in Congress were in the room, Gabby opened her eyes for the first time. (Applause.) Gabby opened her eyes for the first time. (Applause.)

Gabby opened her eyes. Gabby opened her eyes, so I can tell you she knows we are here. She knows we love her. And she knows that we are rooting for her through what is undoubtedly going to be a difficult journey. We are there for her. (Applause.)

Our hearts are full of thanks for that good news, and our hearts are full of gratitude for those who saved others. We are grateful to Daniel Hernandez—(applause)—a volunteer in Gabby's office. (Applause.)

And, Daniel, I'm sorry, you may deny it, but we've decided you are a hero because—(applause)—you ran through the chaos to minister to your boss, and tended to her wounds and helped keep her alive. (Applause.)

We are grateful to the men who tackled the gunman as he stopped to reload. (Applause.) Right over there. (Applause.) We are grateful for petite Patricia Maisch, who wrestled away the killer's ammunition, and undoubtedly saved some lives. (Applause.) And we are grateful for the doctors and nurses and first responders who worked wonders to heal those who'd been hurt. We are grateful to them. (Applause.)

These men and women remind us that heroism is found not only on the fields of battle. They remind us that heroism does not require special training or physical strength. Heroism is here, in the hearts of so many of our fellow citizens, all around us, just waiting to be summoned—as it was on Saturday morning. Their actions, their selflessness poses a challenge to each of us. It raises a question of what, beyond prayers and expressions of concern, is required of us going forward. How can we honor the fallen? How can we be true to their memory?

You see, when a tragedy like this strikes, it is part of our nature to demand explanations—to try and pose some order on the chaos and make sense out of that which seems senseless. Already we've seen a national conversation commence, not only about the motivations behind these killings, but about everything from the merits of gun safety laws to the adequacy of our mental health system. And much of this process, of debating what might be done to prevent such tragedies in the future, is an essential ingredient in our exercise of self-government.

But at a time when our discourse has become so sharply polarized—at a time when we are far too eager to lay the blame for all that ails the world at the feet of those who happen to think differently than we do—it's important for us to pause for a moment and make sure that we're talking with each other in a way that heals, not in a way that wounds. (Applause.)

Scripture tells us that there is evil in the world, and that terrible things happen for reasons that defy human understanding. In the words of Job, "When I looked for light, then came darkness." Bad things happen, and we have to guard against simple explanations in the aftermath.

For the truth is none of us can know exactly what triggered this vicious attack. None of us can know with any certainty what might have stopped these shots from being fired, or what thoughts lurked in the inner recesses of a violent man's mind. Yes, we have to examine all the facts behind this tragedy. We cannot and will not be passive in the face of such violence. We should be willing to challenge old assumptions in order to lessen the prospects of such violence in the future. (Applause.) But what we cannot do is use this tragedy as one more occasion to turn on each other. (Applause.) That we cannot do. (Applause.) That we cannot do.

As we discuss these issues, let each of us do so with a good dose of humility. Rather than pointing fingers or assigning blame, let's use this occasion to expand our moral imaginations, to listen to each other more carefully, to sharpen our instincts for empathy and remind ourselves of all the ways that our hopes and dreams are bound together. (Applause.)

After all, that's what most of us do when we lose somebody in our family—especially if the loss is unexpected. We're shaken out of our routines. We're forced to look inward. We reflect on the past: Did we spend enough time with an aging parent, we wonder. Did we express our gratitude for all the sacrifices that they made for us? Did we tell a spouse just how desperately we loved them, not just once in a while but every single day?

So sudden loss causes us to look backward—but it also forces us to look forward; to reflect on the present and the future, on the manner in which we live our lives and nurture our relationships with those who are still with us. (Applause.)

We may ask ourselves if we've shown enough kindness and generosity and compassion to the people in our lives. Perhaps we question whether we're doing right by our children, or our community, whether our priorities are in order.

We recognize our own mortality, and we are reminded that in the fleeting time we have on this Earth, what matters is not wealth, or status, or power, or fame—but rather, how well we have loved—(applause)—and what small part we have played in making the lives of other people better. (Applause.)

And that process—that process of reflection, of making sure we align our values with our actions—that, I believe, is what a tragedy like this requires.

For those who were harmed, those who were killed—they are part of our family, an American family 300 million strong. (Applause.) We may not have known them personally, but surely we see ourselves in them. In George and Dot, in Dorwan and Mavy, we sense the abiding love we have for our own husbands, our own wives, our own life partners. Phyllis—she's our mom or our grandma; Gabe our brother or son. (Applause.) In Judge Roll, we recognize not only a man who prized his family and doing his job well, but also a man who embodied America's fidelity to the law. (Applause.)

And in Gabby—in Gabby, we see a reflection of our public-spiritedness; that desire to participate in that sometimes frustrating, sometimes contentious, but always necessary and never-ending process to form a more perfect union. (Applause.)

And in Christina—in Christina we see all of our children. So curious, so trusting, so energetic, so full of magic. So deserving of our love. And so deserving of our good example.

If this tragedy prompts reflection and debate—as it should—let's make sure it's worthy of those we have lost. (Applause.) Let's make sure it's not on the usual plane of politics and point-scoring and pettiness that drifts away in the next news cycle.

The loss of these wonderful people should make every one of us strive to be better. To be better in our private lives, to be better friends and neighbors and coworkers and parents. And if, as has been discussed in recent days, their death helps usher in more civility in our public discourse, let us remember it is not because a simple lack of civility caused this tragedy—it did not—but rather because only a more civil and honest public discourse can help us face up to the challenges of our nation in a way that would make them proud. (Applause.)

We should be civil because we want to live up to the example of public servants like John Roll and Gabby Giffords, who knew first and foremost that we are all Americans, and that we can question each other's ideas without questioning each other's love of country and that our task, working together, is to constantly widen the circle of our concern so that we bequeath the American Dream to future generations. (Applause.)

They believed—they believed, and I believe that we can be better. Those who died here, those who saved life here—they help me believe. We may not be able to stop all evil in the world, but I know that how we treat one another, that's entirely up to us. (Applause.)

And I believe that for all our imperfections, we are full of decency and goodness, and that the forces that divide us are not as strong as those that unite us. (Applause.)

That's what I believe, in part because that's what a child like Christina Taylor Green believed. (Applause.)

Imagine—imagine for a moment, here was a young girl who was just becoming aware of our democracy; just beginning to understand the obligations of citizenship; just starting to glimpse the fact that some day she, too, might play a part in shaping her nation's future. She had been elected to her student council. She saw public service as something exciting and hopeful. She was off to meet her congress-woman, someone she was sure was good and important and might be a role model. She saw all this through the eyes of a child, undimmed by the cynicism or vitriol that we adults all too often just take for granted.

I want to live up to her expectations. (Applause.) I want our democracy to be as good as Christina imagined it. I want America to be as good as she imagined it. (Applause.) All of us—we should do everything we can to make sure this country lives up to our children's expectations. (Applause.)

As has already been mentioned, Christina was given to us on September 11th, 2001, one of 50 babies born that day to be pictured in a book called "Faces of Hope." On either side of her photo in that book were simple wishes for a child's life. "I hope you help those in need," read one. "I hope you know all the words to the National Anthem and sing it with your hand over your heart." (Applause.) "I hope you jump in rain puddles."

If there are rain puddles in Heaven, Christina is jumping in them today. (Applause.) And here on this Earth—here on this Earth, we place our hands over our hearts, and we commit ourselves as Americans to forging a country that is forever worthy of her gentle, happy spirit.

May God bless and keep those we've lost in restful and eternal peace. May He love and watch over the survivors. And may He bless the United States of America. (Applause.)

1976 Democratic National Convention Keynote Address

Barbara Jordan
New York, New York
July 12, 1976

Thank you ladies and gentlemen for a very warm reception.

It was one hundred and forty-four years ago that members of the Democratic Party first met in convention to select a Presidential candidate. Since that time, Democrats have continued to convene once every four years and draft a party platform and nominate a Presidential candidate. And our meeting this week is a continuation of that tradition. But there is something different about tonight. There is something special about tonight. What is different? What is special?

I, Barbara Jordan, am a keynote speaker.

A lot of years passed since 1832, and during that time it would have been most unusual for any national political party to ask that a Barbara Jordan to deliver a keynote address. But tonight here I am. And I feel that notwithstanding the past that my presence here is one additional bit of evidence that the American Dream need not forever be deferred.

Now that I have this grand distinction what in the world am I supposed to say? I could easily spend this time praising the accomplishments of this party and attacking the Republicans—but I don't choose to do that. I could list the many problems which Americans have. I could list the problems which cause people to feel cynical, angry, frustrated: problems which include lack of integrity in government; the feeling that the individual no longer counts; the reality of material and spiritual poverty; the feeling that the grand American experiment is failing or has failed. I could recite these problems, and then I could sit down and offer no solutions. But I don't choose to do that either. The citizens of America expect more. They deserve and they want more than a recital of problems.

We are a people in a quandary about the present. We are a people in search of our future. We are a people in search of a national community. We are a people trying not only to solve the problems of the present, unemployment, inflation, but we are attempting on a larger scale to fulfill the promise of America. We are attempting to fulfill our national purpose, to create and sustain a society in which all of us are equal.

Throughout out history, when people have looked for new ways to solve their problems, and to uphold the principles of this nation, many times they have turned to political parties. They have often turned to the Democratic Party. What is it? What is it about the Democratic Party that makes it the instrument the people use when they search for ways to shape their future? Well I believe the answer to that question lies in our concept of governing. Our concept of governing is derived from our view of people. It is a concept deeply rooted in a set of beliefs firmly etched in the national conscience of all of us.

Now what are these beliefs? First, we believe in equality for all and privileges for none. This is a belief that each American regardless of background has equal standing in the public forum—all of us. Because we believe this idea so firmly, we are an inclusive rather than an exclusive party. Let everybody come! I think it no accident that most of those emigrating to America in the 19th century identified with the Democratic Party. We are a heterogeneous party made up of Americans of diverse backgrounds. We believe that the people are the source of all governmental power; that the authority of the people is to be extended, not restricted.

This can be accomplished only by providing each citizen with every opportunity to participate in the management of the government. They must have that, we believe. We believe that the government which represents the authority of all the people, not just one interest group, but all the people, has an obligation to actively—underscore actively—seek to remove those obstacles which would block individual achievement—obstacles emanating from race, sex, economic condition. The government must remove them, seek to remove them.

We are a party of innovation. We do not reject our traditions, but we are willing to adapt to changing circumstances, when change we must. We are willing to suffer the discomfort of change in order to achieve a better future. We have a positive vision of the future founded on the belief that the gap between the promise and reality of America can one day be finally closed.

We believe that.

This, my friends, is the bedrock of our concept of governing. This is a part of the reason why Americans have turned to the Democratic Party. These are the foundations upon which a national community can be built. Let's all understand that these guiding principles cannot be discarded for short-term political gains. They represent what this country is all about. They are indigenous to the American idea. And these are principles which are not negotiable.

In other times, I could stand here and give this kind of exposition on the beliefs of the Democratic Party and that would be enough. But today that is not enough. People want more. That is not sufficient reason for the majority of the people of this country to vote Democratic. We have made mistakes. We realize that. In our haste to do all things for all people, we did not foresee the full consequences of our actions. And when the people raised their voices, we didn't hear. But our deafness was only a temporary condition, and not an irreversible condition.

Even as I stand here and admit that we have made mistakes, I still believe that as the people of America sit in judgment on each party, they will recognize that our mistakes were mistakes of the heart. They'll recognize that.

And now we must look to the future. Let us heed the voice of the people and recognize their common sense. If we do not, we not only blaspheme our political heritage, we ignore the common ties that bind all Americans. Many fear the future. Many are distrustful of their leaders, and believe that their voices are never heard. Many seek only to satisfy their private work wants. To satisfy their private interests. But this is the great danger America faces. That we will cease to be one nation and become instead a collection of interest groups: city against suburb, region against region, individual against individual. Each seeking to satisfy private wants. If that happens, who then will speak for America? Who then will speak for the common good?

This is the question which must be answered in 1976.

Are we to be one people bound together by common spirit, sharing in a common endeavor; or will we become a divided nation? For all of its uncertainty, we cannot flee the future. We must not become the new Puritans and reject our society. We must address and master the future together. It can be done if we restore the belief that we share a sense of national community, that we share a common national endeavor. It can be done.

There is no executive order; there is no law that can require the American people to form a national community. This we must do as individuals, and if we do it as individuals, there is no President of the United States who can veto that decision.

As a first step, we must restore our belief in ourselves. We are a generous people so why can't we be generous with each other? We need to take to heart the words spoken by Thomas Jefferson:

> Let us restore to social intercourse that harmony and affection without which liberty and even life are but dreary things.

A nation is formed by the willingness of each of us to share in the responsibility for upholding the common good. A government is invigorated when each of us is willing to participate in shaping the future of this nation. In this election year we must define the common good and begin again to shape a common future. Let each person do his or her part. If one citizen is unwilling to participate, all of us are going to suffer. For the American idea, though it is shared by all of us, is realized in each one of us.

And now, what are those of us who are elected public officials supposed to do? We call ourselves public servants but I'll tell you this: We as public servants must set an example for the rest of the nation. It is hypocritical for the public official to admonish and exhort the people to uphold the common good if we are derelict in upholding the common good. More is required of public officials than slogans and handshakes and press releases. More is required. We must hold ourselves strictly accountable. We must provide the people with a vision of the future.

If we promise as public officials, we must deliver. If we as public officials propose, we must produce. If we say to the American people it is time for you to be sacrificial; sacrifice. If the public official says that, we [public officials] must be the first to give. We must be. And again, if we make mistakes, we must be willing to admit them. We have to do that. What we have to do is strike a balance between the idea that government should do everything and that idea, the belief, that government ought to do nothing. Strike a balance. Let there be no illusions about the difficulty of forming this kind of a national community. It's tough, difficult, not easy. But a spirit of harmony will survive in America only if each of us remembers that we share a common destiny. If each of us remembers when self-interest and bitterness seem to prevail that we share a common destiny.

I have confidence that we can form this kind of national community.

I have confidence that the Democratic Party can lead the way.

I have that confidence.

We cannot improve on the system of government handed down to us by the founders of the Republic. There is no way to improve upon that. But what we can do is to find new ways to implement that system and realize our destiny.

Now, I began this speech by commenting to you on the uniqueness of a Barbara Jordan making a keynote address. Well I am going to close my speech by quoting a Republican President and I ask you that as you listen to these words of Abraham Lincoln, relate them to the concept of a national community in which every last one of us participates:

> As I would not be a slave, so I would not be a master. This expresses my idea of Democracy. Whatever differs from this, to the extent of the difference, is no Democracy.

Thank you.

Remarks to the U.N.
Fourth World Conference on Women

First Lady Hillary Rodham Clinton
Beijing, China
September 5, 1995

Mrs. Mongella,

Distinguished delegates and guests,

I would like to thank the Secretary General of the United Nations for inviting me to be part of the United Nations Fourth World Conference on Women. This is truly a celebration—a celebration of the contributions women make in every aspect of life: in the home, on the job, in their communities, as mothers, wives, sisters, daughters, learners, workers, citizens and leaders.

It is also a coming together, much the way women come together every day in every country.

We come together in fields and in factories. In village markets and supermarkets. In living rooms and board rooms.

Whether it is while playing with our children in the park or washing clothes in a river, or taking a break at the office water cooler, we come together and talk about our aspirations and concerns. And time and again, our talk turns to our children and our families.

However different we may be, there is far more that unites us than divides us. We share a common future. And we are here to find common ground so that we may help bring new dignity and respect to women and girls all over the world—and in so doing, bring new strength and stability to families as well.

By gathering in Beijing, we are focusing world attention on issues that matter most in the lives of women and their families: access to education, health care, jobs, and credit, the chance to enjoy basic legal and human rights and participate fully in the political life of their countries.

There are some who question the reason for this conference. Let them listen to the voices of women in their homes, neighborhoods, and workplaces.

There are some who wonder whether the lives of women and girls matter to economic and political progress around the globe. ... Let them look at the women gathered here and at Huairou ... the home-makers, nurses, teachers, lawyers, policymakers, and women who run their own businesses.

It is conferences like this that compel governments and peoples everywhere to listen, look and face the world's most pressing problems.

Wasn't it after the women's conference in Nairobi ten years ago that the world focused for the first time on the crisis of domestic violence?

Earlier today, I participated in a World Health Organization forum, where government officials, NGOs, and individual citizens are working on ways to address the health problems of women and girls.

Tomorrow, I will attend a gathering of the United Nations Development Fund for Women. There, the discussion will focus on lo-cal—and highly successful—programs that give hard-working women access to credit so they can improve their own lives and the lives of their families.

What we are learning around the world is that, if women are healthy and educated, their families will flourish. If women are free from vio-lence, their families will flourish. If women have a chance to work and earn as full and equal partners in society, their families will flourish.

And when families flourish, communities and nations will flourish.

That is why every woman, every man, every child, every family, and every nation on our planet has a stake in the discussion that takes place here.

Over the past 25 years, I have worked persistently on issues relating to women, children and families. Over the past two-and-a-half years, I have had the opportunity to learn more about the challenges facing women in my own country and around the world.

I have met new mothers in Jojakarta, Indonesia, who come together regularly in their village to discuss nutrition, family planning, and baby care.

I have met working parents in Denmark who talk about the comfort they feel in knowing that their children can be cared for in creative, safe, and nurturing after-school centers.

I have met women in South Africa who helped lead the struggle to end apartheid and are now helping build a new democracy.

I have met with the leading women of the Western Hemisphere who are working every day to promote literacy and better health care for the children of their countries.

I have met women in India and Bangladesh who are taking out small loans to buy milk cows, rickshaws, thread and other materials to create a livelihood for themselves and their families.

I have met doctors and nurses in Belarus and Ukraine who are trying to keep children alive in the aftermath of Chernobyl.

The great challenge of this conference is to give voice to women everywhere whose experiences go unnoticed, whose words go unheard.

Women comprise more than half the world's population. Women are 70 percent of the world's poor, and two-thirds of those who are not taught to read and write.

Women are the primary caretakers for most of the world's children and elderly. Yet much of the work we do is not valued—not by economists, not by historians, not by popular culture, not by government leaders.

At this very moment, as we sit here, women around the world are giving birth, raising children, cooking meals, washing clothes, cleaning houses, planting crops, working on assembly lines, running companies, and running countries.

Women also are dying from diseases that should have been prevented or treated; they are watching their children succumb to malnutrition caused by poverty and economic deprivation; they are being denied the right to go to school by their own fathers and brothers; they are being forced into prostitution, and they are being barred from the ballot box and the bank lending office.

Those of us who have the opportunity to be here have the responsibility to speak for those who could not.

As an American, I want to speak up for women in my own country—women who are raising children on the minimum wage, women who can't afford health care or child care, women whose lives are threatened by violence, including violence in their own homes.

I want to speak up for mothers who are fighting for good schools, safe neighborhoods, clean air and clean airwaves ... for older women, some of them widows, who have raised their families and now find that their skills and life experiences are not valued in the workplace ... for women who are working all night as nurses, hotel clerks, and fast food chefs so that they can be at home during the day with their kids ... and for women everywhere who simply don't have time to do everything they are called upon to do each day.

Speaking to you today, I speak for them, just as each of us speaks for women around the world who are denied the chance to go to school, or see a doctor, or own property, or have a say about the direction of their lives, simply because they are women.

The truth is that most women around the world work both inside and outside the home, usually by necessity.

We need to understand that there is ho formula for how women should lead their lives. That is why we must respect the choices that each woman makes for herself and her family. Every woman deserves the chance to realize her God-given potential.

We also must recognize that women will never gain full dignity until their human rights are respected and protected.

Our goals for this conference, to strengthen families and societies by empowering women to take greater control over their own destinies, cannot be fully achieved unless all governments—here and around the world—accept their responsibility to protect and promote internationally recognized human rights.

The international community has long acknowledged—and recently affirmed at Vienna—that both women and men are entitled to a range of protections and personal freedoms, from the right of personal security to the right to determine freely the number and spacing of the children they bear.

No one should be forced to remain silent for fear of religious or political persecution, arrest, abuse or torture.

Tragically, women are most often the ones whose human rights are violated. Even in the late 20th century, the rape of women continues to be used as an instrument of armed conflict. Women and children make up a large majority of the world's refugees. And when women are excluded from the political process, they become even more vulnerable to abuse.

I believe that, on the eve of a new millennium, it is time to break our silence. It is time for us to say here in Beijing, and the world to hear, that it is no longer acceptable to discuss women's rights as separate from human rights.

These abuses have continued because, for too long, the history of women has been a history of silence. Even today, there are those who are trying to silence our words.

The voices of this conference and of the women at Huairou must be heard loud and clear:

It is a violation of human rights when babies are denied food, or drowned, or suffocated, or their spines broken, simply because they are born girls.

It is a violation of human rights when women and girls are sold into the slavery of prostitution.

It is a violation of human rights when women are doused with gasoline, set on fire and burned to death because their marriage dowries are deemed too small.

It is a violation of human rights when individual women are raped in their own communities and when thousands of women are subjected to rape as a tactic or prize of war.

It is a violation of human rights when a leading cause of death worldwide among women ages 14 to 44 is the violence they are subjected to in their own homes.

It is a violation of human rights when young girls are brutalized by the painful and degrading practice of genital mutilation.

It is a violation of human rights when women are denied the right to plan their own families, and that includes being forced to have abortions or being sterilized against their will.

If there is one message that echoes forth from this conference, it is that human rights are women's rights. ... And women's rights are human rights.

Let us not forget that among those rights are the right to speak freely. And the right to be heard.

Women must enjoy the right to participate fully in the social and political lives of their countries if we want freedom and democracy to thrive and endure.

It is indefensible that many women in non-governmental organizations who wished to participate in this conference have not been able to attend—or have been prohibited from fully taking part.

Let me be clear. Freedom means the right of people to assemble, organize, and debate openly. It means respecting the views of those who may disagree with the views of their governments. It means not taking citizens away from their loved ones and jailing them, mistreating them, or denying them their freedom or dignity because of the peaceful expression of their ideas and opinions.

In my country, we recently celebrated the 75th anniversary of women's suffrage. It took 150 years after the signing of our Declaration of Independence for women to win the right to vote. It took 72 years of organized struggle on the part of many courageous women and men.

It was one of America's most divisive philosophical wars. But it was also a bloodless war. Suffrage was achieved without a shot fired.

We have also been reminded, in V-J Day observances last weekend, of the good that comes when men and women join together to combat the forces of tyranny and build a better world.

We have seen peace prevail in most places for a half century. We have avoided another world war.

But we have not solved older, deeply-rooted problems that continue to diminish the potential of half the world's population.

Now it is time to act on behalf of women everywhere.

If we take bold steps to better the lives of women, we will be taking bold steps to better the lives of children and families too. Families rely on mothers and wives for emotional support and care; families rely on women for labor in the home; and increasingly, families rely on women for income needed to raise healthy children and care for other relatives.

As long as discrimination and inequities remain so commonplace around the world—as long as girls and women are valued less, fed less, fed last, overworked, underpaid, not schooled and subjected to violence in and out of their homes—the potential of the human family to create a peaceful, prosperous world will not be realized.

Let this conference be our—and the world's—call to action.

And let us heed the call so that we can create a world in which every woman is treated with respect and dignity, every boy and girl is loved and cared for equally, and every family has the hope of a strong and stable future.

Thank you very much.

God's blessings on you, your work and all who will benefit from it.

Endnotes

Part 1

1. William M. Keith and Christian O. Lundberg, *The Essential Guide to Rhetoric* (Boston: Bedford/St. Martin's, 2008), 39.
2. Keith and Lundberg, 39.
3. Ronald A. Heifetz and Martin Linsky, *Leadership on the Line: Staying Alive Through the Dangers of Leading* (Boston: Harvard Business School Press, 2002), 51.
4. Heifetz and Linsky, 53.
5. Heifetz and Linsky, 54.
6. Heifetz and Linsky, 54.
7. Heifetz and Linsky, 53.
8. Heifetz and Linsky, 73.
9. Heifetz and Linsky, 73.
10. Ronald Heifetz, Martin Linsky, and Alexander Grashow, *The Practice of Adaptive Leadership: Tools and Tactics for Changing Your Organization and the World* (Boston: Harvard Business Press, 2009), 178.
11. Jeanette Henderson and Roy Henderson, *There's No Such Thing as Public Speaking* (New York: Prentice Hall, 2007), 107.
12. John Lewis, "The Theodore H. White Lecture on Press and Politics with the Honorable John Lewis," *Harvard Kennedy School Joan Shorenstein Center on the Press, Politics and Public Policy,*

November 20, 2008, http://www.hks.harvard.edu/presspol/news_
events/archive/2008/th_white_lewis_11-20-08.html.

13. "Hillary Clinton Endorses Barack Obama," *The New York Times,*
    June 7, 2008, http://www.nytimes.com/2008/06/07/us/politics/07text-
    clinton.html.

14. Randy Komisar, *The Monk and the Riddle: The Education of a Silicon
    Valley Entrepreneur* (Boston: Harvard Business School Press, 2000),
    83–84.

15. Dan O'Hair, Hannah Rubenstein, and Rob Stewart, *A Pocket Guide
    to Public Speaking,* 3rd ed. (Boston: Bedford/St. Martin's, 2010),
    23–24.

16. Jeanette Henderson and Roy Henderson, *There's No Such Thing
    as Public Speaking,* http://www.theresnosuchthingaspublicspeaking.
    com/index.html.

17. Malcolm Gladwell, *Outliers: The Story of Success* (New York: Little,
    Brown and Company, 2008), 39.

18. Gladwell, 39.

19. Gladwell, 40.

Part 2

1. O'Hair, Rubenstein, and Stewart, 37.

2. O'Hair, Rubenstein, and Stewart, 37.

3. Jonathan Cathèll-Williams, "Speaking in the Storied Sever Hall
   Room 110" (Class Assignment, Harvard Extension School, 2010),
   1–2.

4. Malcolm Gladwell, *Blink: The Power of Thinking Without Thinking*
   (Boston: Little, Brown and Company, 2005), 43–44.

5. Henderson and Henderson, 159–160.

6. Shel Leanne, *Say It Like Obama* (New York: McGraw Hill, 2009),
   39–40.

7. Henderson and Henderson, 196.

8. The greeting discussed in this section is based on ideas in Henderson
   and Henderson, 14–23.

9. Nick Morgan, *Working the Room: How to Move People to Action Through Audience-Centered Speaking* (Boston: Harvard Business School Press, 2003), 194.

10. Leanne, 78.

11. "Bush: 'We Will Do What It Takes,'" *CNN.com*, September 15, 2005, http://www.cnn.com/2005/POLITICS/09/15/bush.transcript.

12. Nick Morgan, "Before You Open Your Mouth," *ChangeThis*, May 6, 2009, http://changethis.com/manifesto/show/58.06.PublicWords.

13. Gail Larsen, *Transformational Speaking: If You Want to Change the World, Tell a Better Story* (Berkeley: Celestial Arts, 2009), 107.

14. Carmine Gallo, "It's Not Your Mouth That Speaks Volumes," *Bloomberg Businessweek*, February 8, 2007, http://www.business week.com/careers/content/feb2007/ca20070207_700175.htm.

Part 3

1. Many of the ideas and examples in Part 3 about the relationship between music and speech appear in Steven D. Cohen et al., "The Music of Speech: Layering Musical Elements to Deliver Powerful Messages," *Relevant Rhetoric: A New Journal of Rhetorical Studies* (Forthcoming).

2. Heifetz and Linsky, 65.

3. Jean Gregg, "Vocal Development and Articulation in Speech and Song," *Journal of Singing* 58.5 (2002): 432.

4. "Bernstein at Harvard," *YouTube*, October 1, 2007, http://www.youtube.com/watch?v=14VhzlcSuT0.

5. Deanna Sellnow and Timothy Sellnow, "The 'Illusion of Life' Rhetorical Perspective: An Integrated Approach to the Study of Music as Communication," *Critical Studies in Media Communication* 18.4 (2001): 397; Susanne Langer, *Feeling and Form* (New York: Charles Scribner's Sons, 1953), 32.

6. Daniel Levitin, *This is Your Brain on Music: The Science of a Human Obsession* (New York: Penguin Group, 2006), 267.

7. Jesse Jackson, "Jesse Jackson Speech to 1988 Democratic National Convention," *American Rhetoric*, July 19, 1988, http://www.americanrhetoric.com/speeches/jessejackson1988dnc.htm.

8. Henderson and Henderson, 126.

9. William Jefferson Clinton, "Oklahoma Bombing Memorial Prayer Service Address," *American Rhetoric*, April 23, 1995, http://www.americanrhetoric.com/speeches/wjcoklahomabombingspeech.htm.

10. Mohandas Gandhi, "Address at Kingsley Hall," *American Rhetoric*, October 17, 1931, http://www.americanrhetoric.com/speeches/mohandasgandhi.htm.

11. O'Hair, Rubenstein, and Stewart, 145.

12. Elizabeth Glaser, "1992 Democratic National Convention Address," *American Rhetoric*, July 14, 1992, http://www.americanrhetoric.com/speeches/elizabethglaser1992dnc.htm.

13. Tom Hanks, "Commencement Address at Vassar College," *American Rhetoric*, May 22, 2005, http://www.americanrhetoric.com/speeches/tomhanksvassar.htm.

14. Henderson and Henderson, 110.

15. These techniques appear in Steven D. Cohen and Thomas E. Wei, "Transmitting Musical Images: Using Music to Teach Public Speaking," *Communication Teacher* 24.3 (2010): 115–121.

16. Aaron Copland, *What to Listen for in Music* (New York: Signet Classics, 2002), 21–22.

17. James C. Humes, *Speak Like Churchill, Stand Like Lincoln* (New York: Three Rivers Press, 2002), 28.

18. Hillary Rodham Clinton, "Remarks to the U.N. 4th World Conference on Women Plenary Session," *American Rhetoric*, September 5, 1995, http://www.americanrhetoric.com/speeches/hillaryclintonbeijingspeech.htm.

19. Philip N. Johnson-Laird and Keith Oatley, "Emotions, Music, and Literature" in *Handbook of Emotions*, edited by Michael Lewis, Jeannette M. Haviland-Jones, and Lisa Feldman Barrett (New York: Guilford Press, 2008), 107.

20. Johnson-Laird and Oatley, 107.

21. Mario Savio, "Sit-in Address on the Steps of Sproul Hall," *American Rhetoric*, December 2, 1964, http://www.americanrhetoric.com/speeches/mariosaviosproulhallsitin.htm.

22. Harry F. Olson, *Music, Physics and Engineering* (New York: Dover Publications, 1967). 36.

23. "In Full: Obama Health Care Address," *YouTube*, September 9, 2009, http://www.youtube.com/watch?v=U1YNF9I25yU.

Part 4

1. Keith and Lundberg, 62.

2. Henderson and Henderson, 117.

3. Leanne, 87.

4. Barack Obama, "2004 Democratic National Convention Keynote Address," *American Rhetoric*, July 27, 2004, http://www.american rhetoric.com/speeches/convention2004/barackobama2004dnc. htm.

5. I first learned about a variation of this activity at a "Brown Bag Discussion on Teaching" at the University of Maryland on March 1, 2010.

6. John Shay, "LABBB" (Class Assignment, Harvard Extension School, 2010), 1.

7. Marshall Ganz, "What is Public Narrative?," *New England Grassroots Environment Fund*, 2008, http://grassrootsfund.org/docs/WhatIsPublicNarrative08.pdf.

8. Collin Ward, "Jasmine" (Class Assignment, Harvard Extension School, 2010), 2.

9. Marshall Ganz, "Notes on Storytelling," *Harvard KSG Practicing Democracy Network*, August 2005, http://www.hks.harvard.edu/organizing/tools/Files/STORYTELLINGNOTES80505.doc.

10. Shay, 1–2.

11. Ganz, "Notes on Storytelling," 6.

12. Keith and Lundberg, 63.

13. Martin Luther King Jr., "I Have a Dream," *American Rhetoric*, August 28, 1963, http://www.americanrhetoric.com/speeches/mlkihaveadream.htm.

14. "Barack Obama's Acceptance Speech," *The New York Times*, August 28, 2008, http://www.nytimes.com/2008/08/28/us/politics/28text-obama.html?pagewanted=all.

15. Lyndon Baines Johnson, "We Shall Overcome," *American Rhetoric*, March 15, 1965, http://www.americanrhetoric.com/speeches/lbjweshallovercome.htm.

16. Ronald Reagan, "First Inaugural Address," *American Rhetoric*, January 20, 1981, http://www.americanrhetoric.com/speeches/ronaldreagandfirstinaugural.html.

17. Emily Guadagnoli, "Know More" (Class Assignment, Harvard Extension School, 2010), 1–3.

18. Guadagnoli, 4.

Part 5

1. Richard Zeoli, *The 7 Principles of Public Speaking: Proven Methods from a PR Professional* (New York: Skyhorse Publishing, 2008), 153.

2. Leanne, 80.

3. These frameworks are based on ideas in "Impromptu Speaking (Table Topics)," *Toastmasters New Zealand*, http://www.toastmasters.org.nz/index.cfm/Speaking_Resources/Table_Topics.html.

4. O'Hair, Rubenstein, and Stewart, 189.

5. Laura Miller, "Far from Narnia," *New Yorker*, December 26, 2005, http://www.newyorker.com/archive/2005/12/26/051226fa_fact.

6. Douglas M. Fraleigh and Joseph S. Tuman, *Speak Up!: An Illustrated Guide to Public Speaking* (Boston: Bedford/St. Martin's, 2009), 172.

7. This speech excerpt is an edited version of material in Amy DePalma, "Public Relations Proposal for Increased Recycling Within Lakewood, Ohio," *Amy DePalma Portfolio*, December 18, 2009, http://www.amydepalma.com/works/print/recycling/proposal.pdf.

8. Henderson and Henderson, 48.

9. "Child Passenger Safety: Fact-Sheet," *Centers for Disease Control and Prevention*, February 2, 2010, http://www.cdc.gov/ncipc/factsheets/childpas.htm.

10. This speech excerpt is an edited version of material in "Child Passenger Survey (CPS)," *The State of New Jersey*, http://www.state.nj.us/oag/hts/childseats/index.html.

11. "Frequently Asked Questions," *Environmental Working Group*, http://www.foodnews.org/faq.php.

12. This speech excerpt is an edited version of material in http://www.foodnews.org/faq.php.

13. J. Lyman MacInnis, *The Elements of Great Public Speaking: How to Be Calm, Confident, and Compelling* (Berkeley: Ten Speed Press, 2006), 56.

14. O'Hair, Rubenstein, and Stewart, 222.

15. James M. Kouzes and Barry Z. Posner, *The Leadership Challenge*, 4th ed. (San Francisco: Jossey-Bass, 2007), 133.

16. Carmine Gallo, "How to Inspire People Like Obama Does," *Bloomberg Businessweek*, March 3, 2008, http://www.businessweek.com/smallbiz/content/mar2008/sb2008033_156351.htm.

17. James M. Kouzes and Barry Z. Posner, *The Leadership Challenge*, 2nd ed. (San Francisco: Jossey-Bass, 1995), 143–144.

18. "Barack Obama's New Hampshire Primary Speech," *The New York Times*, January 8, 2008, http://www.nytimes.com/2008/01/08/us/politics/08text-obama.html?pagewanted=all.

19. Kouzes and Posner, 2nd ed., 139.

20. J.K. Rowling, "The Fringe Benefits of Failure, and the Importance of Imagination," *Harvard Magazine*, June 5, 2008, http://harvardmagazine.com/commencement/the-fringe-benefits-failure-the-importance-imagination.

Index

"10,000-Hour Rule," 24

A

acceptance, 37
acknowledgment, 37
acting like a leader, 4, 35–36
addressing a related topic, 101–102
Aeschylus, 121
alliteration, 88
anaphora, 85–87
anecdotes
    characters, 79–80
    key to, 77
    moral, 82–83
    plot, 80–82
    setting, 78–79
approaching your audience, 37
Aristotle, 128
art of practice, xv
    example of Reagan, 23–24
    opportunities, 25
    time needed for mastery, 24–25
assessments, constant, 6
attire, selecting, 35
audience
    connecting with, xvi
    creating strong bond with, 39–44
    feeling of access to you, 45–46
    focusing on one member of, 46

    knowing your, 29–31
    respecting values of, 21
    steps in greeting, 37–38
audience analysis, 29–31
audience-centered approach, 29
authority, projecting, 34–36

B

balcony. *See* getting on the balcony
Bax, Arnold, 60, 61
Beethoven, Ludwig van, 65, 66
believing in your message, 113–116
Bernstein, Elmer, 66
Bernstein, Leonard, 51
Billy the Kid (Copland), 62
breaking up the question, 97–99
breaking your goal into logical steps,
    113
building to climax, 67–68
Bush, George W., 40, 123

C

championing your cause
    addressing three key questions,
    16–18
    embracing difficult topics, 20–21
    finding your passion, 18–19

importance of persistence in, 15–16
characters (in anecdote), 79–80
charisma, 36
clasping your hands, 9, 10
Clinton, Bill, 59, 131–133
Clinton, Hillary, 16–18, 66, 149–155
closing the loop, 89–91
clothing, selecting, 35
conflicting values, 21
controversial topics. *See* difficult topics
Copland, Aaron, 62
creating a moment, 77
creating a strong bond
  highlighting the relevance, 39, 42–44
  referencing present, 41–42
  showing care for audience, 39
  using inclusive words, 40–41, 134–135
credibility
  enhancing, 37–38, 42
  establishing, 3–4
customizing your message, 105–106

D

Death and Transfiguration (Strauss), 58, 61
default public speaking settings
  eliminating filler words, 12–13
  identifying, 9–10
  overcoming nervousness, 10–11
  using natural gestures, 13–14
default settings. *See* default public speaking settings
deferring the topic, 101
descriptive words, 74
details
  addressing in follow-ups, 95
  providing the, 96–97
  thin-slicing and, 34
  using for clear picture, 78, 79–80

difficult topics, embracing, 20–21
discussion questions, 26, 47, 69, 92, 117
dressing one step up. *See* selecting an outfit
drive versus passion, 18
dynamics, 59–60

E

easing into eye contact, 11
embracing difficult topics, 20–21
emotion, evoking, 66–67
empathetic identification, 79
enhancing credibility, 37–38, 42
enhancing your image, 36
epistrophe, 87
The Essential Guide to Rhetoric (Keith and Lundberg), 3–4
ethos, establishing positive, 3–4
evaluations, constant, 6
evoking emotion, 66–67
exercises, to overcome nervousness, 10–11
exploring a potential solution, 106–107
extemporaneous speeches. *See* impromptu speeches
eye contact, 11, 35

F

feelings, expressing through music of speech, 51–52
filler word hot spots, 12
filler words, eliminating, 12–13
finding your passion, 18–19
five key musical elements
  dynamics, 59–60
  pitch, 60–61
  rhythm, 62–63
  tempo, 58–59
  timbre, 61–62
  using, 57

Flight of the Bumblebee (Rimsky-Korsakov), 58
Fraleigh, Douglas, 104–105
framing your issue as a problem. *See* identifying a narrow problem

G

Gallo, Carmine, 45, 111
Gandhi, Mohandas, 60
Ganz, Marshall, 79, 80, 82
gestures. *See* natural gestures
getting lost in your message, 113–114
getting on the balcony, 5–7
Gladwell, Malcolm, 24, 33–34
Glaser, Elizabeth, 61
"The Great Communicator," 24
greeting your audience, 37–38
Gregg, Jean, 51
Gun Battle (Copland: *Billy the Kid*), 62

H

hand gestures. *See* natural gestures
Hanks, Tom, 62–63
Harry Potter series (Rowling), 114
Heifetz, Ronald, 5–7, 51
Henderson, Jeanette, 14, 23, 35, 36, 58, 63, 74, 106
Henderson, Roy, 14, 23, 35, 36, 58, 63, 74, 106
highlighting the relevance, 39, 42–44
historical success anecdotes, 111–113
holding out hope, 110–111
Holst, Gustav, 62, 66
hot spots for filler words, 12
Humes, James, 66

I

identifying a narrow problem, 104–106
"I Have a Dream" (King), 57, 86
imagery, 74–75
impromptu speeches
  breaking up the question framework, 97–99
  providing the details framework, 96–97
  shifting the focus framework, 101–102
  shrinking the topic framework, 99–100
  staying on message, 95
inclusive words, using, 40–41
inflection points, 80–81
inspirational speeches
  believing in your message, 113–116
  defining, 109–110
  examples, 143–147, 149–155
  holding out hope, 110–111
  making impossible possible, 111–113
introducing a specific action, 107–108
introductions, importance of, 36

J

Jackson, Jesse, 58
Johnson, Lyndon, 87

K

Keith, William, 3–4, 73, 85
Kennedy, John F., 125–130
Kennedy, Robert F., 121–122
King, Martin Luther, Jr., 57, 86, 121–122
knowing your audience, 29–31
Komisar, Randy, 18

CPSIA information can be obtained at www.ICGtesting.com
Printed in the USA
BVOW04s0656250714

360462BV00009B/360/P